THE CLASSIC
SOUTH AFRICAN
COOKBOOK

MELINDA ROODT

Published in 2016 by Struik Lifestyle
(an imprint of Penguin Random House South Africa Pty Ltd)
Company Reg. No. 1953/000441/07
No. 4 The Estuaries, Oxbow Crescent, Century Avenue, Century City, 7441
PO Box 1144, Cape Town 8000, South Africa

www.randomstruik.co.za

First edition published in 2016 by Struik Lifestyle

ISBN 978-1-43230-673-1

Publisher: Linda de Villiers
Managing editor: Cecilia Barfield
Design manager: Beverley Dodd
Editor: Bronwen Maynier
Designer: Beverley Dodd
Photographer: Christin Boggs-Peyper
Author photo: Jo Spies
Author hair and makeup: Tamaryn Pretorius
Contributing photographers: Yolandie Janse van Rensburg, Gernando Roodt, Marianne Hattingh, Corné van Eck and Thelna Esterhuizen
Stylists: Melinda Roodt and Marianne Hattingh
Proofreader and indexer: Pat Barton

Reproduction by Hirt & Carter Cape (Pty) Ltd
Printing and binding by in China RR Donnelley Asia Printing Solutions Ltd

Also available in Afrikaans as
    Die Klassieke Suid-Afrikaanse Kookboek
ISBN: 978-1-43230-674-8

MIX
Paper from responsible sources
FSC® C101537
www.fsc.org

CONTENTS

INTRODUCTION

I have had a passion for good food for as long as I can remember. My childhood memories are filled with scenes of big family celebrations. And we were a BIG family indeed, as from the eight children born to my paternal grandparents, there came twenty-eight grandchildren, and so a family braai was no small occasion.

I have fond memories of the warmth of home-baked bread straight from the AGA coal stove; the large table in my grandmother's kitchen where our parents would sit all night; the smell of freshly baked scones made by my maternal grandmother; and the bell that rang to signal that it was meal time.

After getting married and going into ministry, our first church was in a small town in the Orange Free State, where I learnt many secrets first hand in the farm kitchens. As we were not always able to eat out, I learnt over the years to cook better food at home than what you would find in a local restaurant.

Just before my dearest friend Truda van Heerden immigrated to Australia, she asked me for a few recipes that would remind her of home once overseas. I began by writing them down in a book for her, but soon realised that there was a need generally among many of my friends for recipes for simple and nutritious home-cooked meals. And so I started hosting cooking schools in my home, and for eighteen months I inspired women to cook good food at home, rather than to eat out or buy takeaways.

After all, a good home-cooked meal not only brings family and friends together; it allows them to share in one another's lives. A good meal is the heart of the home, and we tend to underestimate its potential value. The dinner table is a safe place for family members to look one another in the eye and share about their day. It is a place where children and parents can connect and communicate. This is priceless, as communication forms the foundation for any relationship. Over a good meal in the comfort of your own home you can not only connect with those you love, but get to know others better. When we have people over, we always have good food. The two dining tables in my home, one inside and one outside, have become the centrepieces of our life.

With this book I hope to inspire you to create that place of loving, sharing and connecting over food in your own home. Food is about more than just cooking; it is about creating memories that will linger for years to come. Food feeds the body, but good food feeds the soul!

I want to thank you, Truda my friend, for believing in me and for challenging me beyond my own limitations.

I want to thank my family, whose passion for food has grown with my own and who have journeyed through all the tastings and celebrations with me.

The Classic South African Cookbook is a compilation of recipes from my own kitchen, from friends and from recipes I have collected over the years.

MELINDA ROODT

Food not only feeds the body but, like music, it feeds the soul.

Expectation: Today is a new day,
expect something good to happen to you!

BREAKFASTS

Over weekends we go big on breakfast as the whole family is at home and we usually cook together. We serve breakfast at the table, either on the porch or inside, and enjoy the feeling of togetherness over steaming cappuccinos.

CREAMY SCRAMBLED EGGS
and crispy bacon

SERVES 4

15 ml olive oil

250 g rindless streaky bacon

8 extra-large eggs

2 egg yolks

salt and freshly ground black
    pepper to taste

5 ml butter

1. Heat a frying pan over medium-high heat and add the olive oil.
2. Quickly fry the bacon strips on each side until slightly golden, then turn down the heat and slowly fry until most of the fat has been rendered.
3. When the bacon becomes crispy, drain off the fat, place the strips on paper towel and keep warm.
4. In a mixing bowl, beat the whole eggs and egg yolks and season with salt and pepper.
5. Melt the butter over medium heat in a clean frying pan.
6. As soon as the butter starts to bubble, add the eggs and leave until the edges begin to set.
7. With a wooden spoon, push the egg at the edges towards the middle.
8. Keep gently pushing the spoon through the eggs until the eggs are cooked but still moist. Do not overcook, or they will become dry.
9. Serve immediately with the crispy bacon.

This is breakfast at its best! Serve with fresh ciabatta or croissants.

POACHED EGG ON SPINACH AND TOASTED BAGUETTE
with tomato relish

15 ml olive oil

4 handfuls baby spinach leaves

15 ml vinegar

4 slices baguette (see page 79)

4 extra-large eggs

butter to serve

TOMATO RELISH

15 ml olive oil

1 onion, diced

2 large tomatoes, diced

45 ml chutney

salt and freshly ground black
    pepper to taste

1. To make the tomato relish, heat the olive oil in a medium frying pan.
2. Sauté the onion until cooked.
3. Add the tomatoes and fry until cooked.
4. Add the chutney and season to taste. Keep warm while you prepare the spinach and eggs.
5. In a separate frying pan, heat the olive oil and sauté the spinach leaves until just wilted, then season with salt and set aside.
6. Bring 1 litre of water to the boil in a medium saucepan, then turn down the heat to a simmer and add the vinegar.
7. Place the baguette slices in the toaster to toast.
8. While the bread is toasting, gently break the eggs one by one into the pan of simmering water. Poach for 3–4 minutes (for medium) until the egg whites are set.
9. Gently remove each egg with a slotted spoon and place on paper towel to drain.
10. Butter the toasted baguette slices and place a quarter of the spinach on each slice. Place an egg on top, season with salt and pepper and serve immediately with the warm tomato relish.

When poached to medium, the eggs should ooze over the bread and spinach when you cut into them. It may seem tricky to poach eggs, but after the third try you should be able to do it perfectly. And remember, good poached eggs should not taste of vinegar!

BREAKFAST FRITTATA

SERVES 4

15 ml butter

½ onion, finely diced

½ red pepper, finely diced

4–5 rashers rindless
    bacon, diced

5 eggs

60 ml milk

salt and freshly ground black
    pepper to taste

60 ml grated Parmesan cheese

15 ml chopped fresh parsley

250 ml grated mozzarella or
    provolone cheese

fresh parsley to garnish

1. Preheat the oven to 180 °C.
2. Melt the butter over low heat in a medium ovenproof frying pan.
3. Add the onion and red pepper and sauté over medium heat.
4. Add the bacon and fry until crispy.
5. Whisk the eggs and milk in a medium bowl and season with salt and pepper.
6. Add the Parmesan cheese and chopped parsley to the eggs.
7. Mix well and pour the egg mixture into the pan, keeping it over medium–low heat.
8. Leave the pan until the egg starts to set slightly around the edges.
9. Using a spatula, gently push the egg on the edges to the middle of the pan. Swirl the pan to make sure the runny egg covers the base.
10. When the egg is half cooked, place the pan in the oven and bake for about 5 minutes until the frittata is cooked.
11. Sprinkle over the mozzarella or provolone cheese and garnish with fresh parsley.
12. Cut the frittata into wedges and serve straight from the pan with fresh bread rolls or toast.

FRENCH TOAST
with berry compote and crème fraiche

SERVES 4–6

6–8 extra-large eggs

a pinch of salt

30–45 ml sunflower oil

30–45 ml butter

8–12 slices ciabatta bread
  (see page 80)

250 g crème fraiche

BERRY COMPOTE

400 g frozen berries

125 ml white sugar

5 ml lemon juice

a pinch of salt

1. Preheat the oven to 140 °C.
2. Bring all the ingredients for the berry compote to the boil in a medium saucepan.
3. Stir, then turn down the heat and simmer until slightly thickened and the sugar has melted. Remove from the heat and set aside.
4. Beat the eggs with the pinch of salt in a medium shallow bowl.
5. Place a large frying pan over medium heat, add the oil and butter and heat until it starts to froth.
6. Submerge one slice of bread at a time in the beaten egg, gently lift it out and allow the excess egg to drip off before placing the slice in the pan.
7. Fry for 2–3 minutes on each side until golden brown.
8. Lift out onto a plate lined with paper towel and keep warm in the oven until all the bread is done.
9. Serve the French toast with the warm berry compote and dollops of crème fraiche.

This is definitely not your everyday breakfast, but it's a sure winner for those special days – truly decadent!

KRUMMELPAP

500 ml water
5 ml salt
625 ml good-quality unbleached maize meal
30–45 ml butter

1. Place a medium saucepan over high heat, add the water and salt and bring to the boil.
2. Pour in all the maize meal at once, cover the pan with a lid and turn down the heat to its lowest setting.
3. Cook for 10 minutes before stirring with a fork until the mixture resembles coarse crumbs. Work out all the big lumps and cover again with the lid.
4. Continue to cook for a further 30–45 minutes, stirring every 10 minutes.
5. Just before serving, stir in the butter and serve hot.

In my aunt's kitchen on the farm, *krummelpap* was served with fresh warm milk straight from the dairy and enough sugar for crunch ... *Krummelpap*, or putu pap as it is called in the African tradition, is a firm staple but also a favourite of our nation. This recipe can be easily doubled. Serve with milk and sugar for breakfast, or with tomato and onion sauce for a braai (see page 310). I buy a good-quality unbleached maize meal from our local mill.

BUTTERMILK PANCAKES
with maple syrup

SERVES 4

375 ml buttermilk

1 extra-large egg

250 ml cake flour

5 ml baking powder

1.25 ml salt

15 ml butter

maple syrup to serve

cream to serve

1. Using a whisk or electric mixer, combine the buttermilk and egg in a large bowl.
2. Sift in the cake flour, baking powder and salt and mix well.
3. Melt the butter in a large frying pan over medium heat.
4. When the butter starts to bubble, pour the batter into the pan to create pancakes of the desired size.
5. Cook until bubbles form and burst on the surface of the pancakes, then flip them over and cook on the other side until browned.
6. Keep the cooked pancakes in a heated serving dish until all the batter has been used up.
7. Serve with maple syrup and cream. For variation add chopped nuts or fresh fruit.

These pancakes/flapjacks are really rich. The batter does not contain any sugar, so you can smother them with syrup. These are delicious served with crispy bacon strips on the side.

Buttermilk SCONES

100 g butter

500 ml cake flour

15 ml baking powder

2.5 ml salt

30 ml white sugar

1 extra-large egg

180 ml buttermilk

butter, grated cheese, jam and
cream to serve

1. Preheat the oven to 200 °C.
2. Place the oven rack one shelf above the middle and grease a baking tray.
3. Cut the butter into 1 cm cubes and place in the freezer for 10 minutes.
4. In a mixing bowl, sift together the flour, baking powder, salt and sugar, twice.
5. Add the butter to the dry ingredients and cut it through the flour by hand, with a dough knife or with an electric mixer (K-mixer) until it resembles coarse crumbs.
6. In a separate bowl, beat the egg well and then add the buttermilk.
7. Pour the liquid into the flour mixture and mix until just combined. It should still be a little crumbly at the bottom. Do not overmix, otherwise the dough will become tough.
8. Turn out onto a well-floured surface and bring the dough together with your hands. Fold the edges over towards the middle.
9. Using a floured rolling pin, roll the dough into a 2 cm thick rectangle.
10. Fold the ends of the rectangle towards the middle and roll out again to 2 cm thick. Repeat this rolling and folding action four times.
11. Finally, roll out the dough to 2 cm thick and gently press out rounds with a 4–5 cm scone cutter.
12. Place the scones on the greased baking tray and bake for 12–15 minutes.
13. Serve warm with butter, grated cheese, jam and cream.

We absolutely love these scones and sometimes enjoy them as a side to our breakfast instead of bread, though they are just as good on their own. By folding and rolling the dough, you create layers within the scone. This allows the cold butter to form little air pockets in the dough – the secret to a perfect scone. The scone should then break in half perfectly by hand.

Chocolate MUFFINS

375 ml cake flour

125 ml white sugar

5 ml baking powder

2.5 ml bicarbonate of soda

45 ml cocoa powder

1 ml salt

2 extra-large eggs

180 ml buttermilk

60 ml sunflower oil

180 ml chocolate chips

1. Preheat the oven to 200 °C.
2. Place the oven rack one shelf above the middle and grease two six-cup muffin tins.
3. Sift all the dry ingredients into a mixing bowl.
4. In a separate bowl, lightly whisk the eggs, then add the buttermilk and oil and mix well.
5. Fold the liquid into the flour mixture until combined.
6. Fold in the chocolate chips.
7. Spoon the mixture into the muffin tins, filling each cup about three-quarters full.
8. Bake for 12–15 minutes, until a skewer inserted into the centre of a muffin comes out clean.
9. Remove the muffins from the tins and cool them on a wire rack before storing in an airtight container for up to three days.

These muffins are ideal when you need to pack breakfast on the go.

Cranberry and almond MUFFINS

375 ml cake flour

60 ml white sugar

5 ml baking powder

1 ml salt

2.5 ml bicarbonate of soda

45 ml milk

1 extra-large egg

250 ml full-cream plain yoghurt

45 ml sunflower oil

100 ml dried cranberries,
   roughly chopped

30 g flaked almonds

1. Preheat the oven to 200 ˚C.
2. Place the oven rack one shelf above the middle and grease two six-cup muffin tins.
3. Sift the flour, sugar, baking powder and salt into a mixing bowl.
4. Mix the bicarbonate of soda into the milk.
5. In a separate bowl, whisk the egg, then add the yoghurt, oil and milk and mix well.
6. Fold the liquid into the flour mixture until combined.
7. Fold in the cranberries.
8. Spoon the mixture into the muffin tins, filling each cup about three-quarters full.
9. Sprinkle some flaked almonds over each muffin.
10. Bake for 12–15 minutes until a skewer inserted into the centre of a muffin comes out clean.
11. Remove the muffins from the tins and cool on a wire rack before storing in an airtight container for up to three days.

VARIATIONS:

Cheese and parsley muffins
Replace the salt, sugar, cranberries and almonds with: 5 ml salt, 250 ml grated Cheddar cheese and 30 ml finely chopped fresh parsley.

Cappuccino muffins
Replace the cranberries and almonds with: 30 ml instant coffee granules and 180 ml chocolate chips.

Date and nut muffins
Replace the cranberries and almonds with: 125 ml chopped dates and 125 ml chopped walnuts or pecans.

These are not too sweet and are ideal for breakfast.

Homemade
MUESLI

MAKES ABOUT 500 G

200 g oats
100 g sunflower seeds
100 g pumpkin seeds
50 g sesame seeds
50 g linseeds
200 g honey

1. Preheat the oven to 200 °C.
2. Place the oven rack one shelf above the middle.
3. Mix all the dry ingredients and spread out the mixture on a large baking tray.
4. Bake for 20 minutes.
5. Remove from the oven and pour the honey over the toasted muesli. Mix well and spread the mixture over the entire tray.
6. Bake for another 20 minutes.
7. Remove from the oven and allow to cool.
8. Loosen the muesli with a fork and store in an airtight container. It will keep for up to one month.

Enjoy this muesli with honey, fresh fruit and yoghurt of your choice.

Strawberry
SMOOTHIE

250 g strawberries
250 ml plain yoghurt
30 ml honey

1. Place all the ingredients in a blender and blend until smooth.
2. If it is too thick, add 30–60 ml cold water and blend.
3. Serve immediately.

This is a fresh and light breakfast for a warm summer morning.
You can substitute the strawberries with any other fruit you like.

Forgiveness: Forgive, so that you can put the past behind you, embrace today and look forward to tomorrow!

STARTERS

With the wonderful weather we have in South Africa in summer, we can enjoy long evenings of braais and visiting family and friends. As we all know, the real cooking of the meat never starts early, and so starters are the best way to keep your famished guests' appetites at bay and also stretch out the evening.

Basil pesto
PASTRY DISCS

MAKES 50–60

400 g roll readymade puff
  pastry
± 80 ml cake flour for flouring
70 g basil pesto (see page 302)
125 ml finely grated Parmesan
  cheese

1. Preheat the oven to 200 °C on the thermo-fan setting* and grease a baking tray.
2. Roll out the puff pastry on a well-floured surface into a rectangle about a third bigger than its original size.
3. Spread the basil pesto over the rolled-out pastry.
4. Cut the rectangle in half to make two smaller rectangles and roll up each from the short side to form cylinders.
5. Cut into circles about 0.5 cm thick and place on the baking tray, facing up.
6. Sprinkle some Parmesan cheese on top of each and bake for 12–15 minutes until the pastry is cooked.
7. Serve warm.

* While a thermo-fan oven is preferable, a conventional oven will also work.

Make your own basil pesto using the recipe on page 302, and then make these quick and easy delights.

BLINIS
with salmon and crème fraiche

250 ml cake flour

5 ml baking powder

2.5 ml salt

180 ml milk

1 extra-large egg

15 ml melted butter

about 65 g butter to cook

250 g fresh salmon

250 g crème fraiche

a handful of fresh dill to serve

1. Sift the flour, baking powder and salt into a bowl.
2. In a separate bowl, combine the milk, egg and melted butter.
3. Add the liquid to the flour and mix well to form a smooth batter.
4. Heat 15–30 ml of the 65 g butter in a large frying pan until it froths.
5. Drop spoonfuls of batter into the pan to make small, bite-sized blinis.
6. Cook the blinis over medium heat until the bubbles in the batter burst, then turn over and cook on the other side until golden.
7. Turn out onto a serving plate and repeat until you have used up all the batter.
8. Cut the salmon into very thin slices, 3–4 cm long, and roll each into a small rose.
9. Place a dollop of crème fraiche onto each blini and top with a salmon rose.
10. Garnish with a sprig of fresh dill and serve immediately.

This canapé is ideal for sushi lovers. The blinis can be made a few hours in advance and kept in an airtight container. Garnish with the salmon, crème fraiche and dill just before serving.

BRUSCHETTA
with basil pesto and Parmesan

50 cm Italian-style baguette
   (see page 79)
30 ml olive oil
125 ml basil pesto
   (see page 302)
125 ml finely grated Parmesan
   cheese
13 cherry tomatoes, halved
a few fresh basil leaves
   to garnish

1. Preheat the oven's grill.
2. Cut the baguette into slices 0.5–1 cm thick and place on a baking tray.
3. Toast the bread on the highest oven rack under the grill for a minute on each side until golden.
4. Using a pastry brush, brush the top of each bruschetta with olive oil.
5. Spread 5 ml basil pesto onto each bruschetta and garnish with 5 ml Parmesan cheese. Top each with a cherry tomato half.
6. Place the bruschetta on a serving board and garnish the board with basil leaves.
7. Serve immediately.

Bruschetta is the Italian name for grilled bread topped with garlic and/or pesto.

Camembert and
FIG PARCELS

MAKES 8

4 sheets phyllo pastry

100 g butter, melted

125 g round Camembert
   cheese

220 g sundried preserved
   figs, halved

chopped fresh thyme to taste

8 fresh chives

8 fresh figs

8 sprigs fresh thyme

1. Preheat the oven to 160 °C and spray a baking tray with non-stick cooking spray.
2. Cut the phyllo pastry sheets into 20 cm squares. Keep them covered with a clean damp cloth to prevent the pastry from drying out while you work.
3. Place a pastry square on a clean surface and, using a pastry brush, brush with melted butter. Place another square of pastry on top and brush this too with melted butter.
4. Cut the Camembert into eight equal pieces and place one piece in the middle of the pastry square.
5. Place half a preserved fig on top of the cheese and sprinkle over some thyme.
6. Bring the corners of the phyllo together to form a small parcel, twist the pastry to close the parcel and place on the baking tray.
7. Brush the outside with melted butter.
8. Repeat with the remaining ingredients until you have eight phyllo parcels.
9. Bake for 12–15 minutes until the pastry is golden brown.
10. Tie a chive around the top of each parcel like a ribbon and serve with fresh figs and sprigs of fresh thyme.

This starter is a decadent delight and can be served at any glamorous affair.

Cheese and
HERB STRAWS

MAKES 15–20

400 g roll puff pastry
± 80 ml cake flour for flouring
30 ml dried Italian herbs
375 ml grated Cheddar cheese

1. Preheat the oven to 200 °C on the thermo-fan setting* and spray a baking tray with non-stick cooking spray.
2. Unroll the pastry onto a well-floured surface.
3. Evenly sprinkle the herbs over the whole rectangle of pastry.
4. Evenly sprinkle the cheese over half of the rectangle.
5. Fold the plain half over the half with cheese and roll lightly with a rolling pin to compress the two layers.
6. Cut into strips 10 cm long and 1 cm wide and twist each into a tight spiral.
7. Place on the baking tray 3 cm apart and bake for 12–15 minutes until golden brown. Allow to cool slightly before serving.

* While a thermo-fan oven is preferable, a conventional oven will also work.

Never buy store-bought cheese straws as homemade ones are the best when served still slightly warm, and they're really easy to make.

Crumbed PRAWNS

24 pink prawn tails
125 ml cake flour
salt to taste
250 ml breadcrumbs, toasted
3 extra-large eggs
750 ml sunflower oil
125 ml salad cream

1. Clean and devein the prawn tails, leaving the end bit of tail intact.
2. Place the flour in a bowl and season with salt.
3. Place the breadcrumbs in a separate bowl.
4. Beat the eggs in a third bowl.
5. Heat the oil in a medium saucepan over high heat.
6. Roll each prawn in the flour, then in the beaten egg, and finally in the breadcrumbs.
7. Carefully lower 5–6 of the prawns into the hot oil at a time and cook for about 2 minutes.
8. Remove with a slotted spoon and drain on paper towel.
9. Repeat until all the prawns are cooked, then transfer to a serving dish and serve with the salad cream as a dip.

Serve these with salad cream, not mayonnaise; it makes for a creamier dip.

Mealie and CHEESE CROQUETTES

375 ml water

2.5 ml salt

125 ml good-quality
    mealie meal

2 large eggs

125 ml cake flour

250 ml grated Cheddar cheese

10 ml baking powder

5 ml butter

500 ml sunflower oil

rosemary salt to taste

1. Bring the water and salt to the boil in a medium saucepan with a tight-fitting lid.
2. Add the mealie meal and briskly stir with a whisk until all the lumps have dissolved. Do not add the mealie meal if the water is bubbling vigorously. If it is, remove the pan from the heat until it stops, turn down the heat and then add the mealie meal.
3. Put on the lid, turn the heat to low and cook for 30 minutes, stirring once or twice with a wooden spoon.
4. Place the cooked mealie meal in a large bowl and allow to cool slightly.
5. Mix in the eggs, followed by the flour, cheese, baking powder and butter. Mix well until all the lumps have been removed.
6. Heat the oil in a large frying pan.
7. Carefully drop teaspoonfuls of batter into the hot oil and fry for 1–2 minutes per side until cooked.
8. Remove from the oil with a slotted spoon and drain on paper towel.
9. Season with rosemary salt and serve warm.

These make the ideal starter at a braai. Make your own rosemary salt by finely chopping fresh rosemary leaves, adding coarse salt and chopping them together until well combined.

Spinach and feta
PHYLLO ROLLS

MAKES 15

15 ml olive oil

1 onion, finely diced

300 g baby spinach leaves

200 g plain feta cheese,
    crumbled

30 ml breadcrumbs

30 ml plain cottage cheese

salt and freshly ground black
    pepper to taste

3 sheets phyllo pastry

30 ml melted butter

sweet chilli sauce to serve

1. Preheat the oven to 180 °C and spray a baking tray with non-stick cooking spray.
2. Heat the olive oil in a small frying pan and sauté the onion until cooked. Remove the onion from the pan and set aside.
3. In the same pan, fry the spinach leaves over high heat until they turn bright green. Remove from the pan to cool.
4. In a mixing bowl, combine the onion, cooled spinach, feta cheese, breadcrumbs and cottage cheese. Season to taste.
5. Place a sheet of phyllo pastry on a clean surface. (Keep the remaining phyllo sheets under a clean damp cloth while you work, to prevent them from drying out.)
6. Using a pastry brush, brush the sheet of pastry with melted butter and cut the sheet into 12 x 16 cm rectangles.
7. Taking one rectangle, place a tablespoon of the spinach mixture in a line at the short end.
8. Fold over the long sides and then roll up the pastry like a cigar, starting at the short end with the filling.
9. Brush with butter and place on the baking tray.
10. Repeat with the remaining rectangles and sheets of pastry until you have used up all the filling.
11. Space the spring rolls 3 cm apart on the baking tray and bake for 20 minutes.
12. Allow to cool slightly before serving with sweet chilli sauce as a dip.

This new take on spring rolls is a firm favourite.

STEAMED BROCCOLI AND ASPARAGUS
with avocado dip

150 g tenderstem broccoli

150 g fresh asparagus

fresh lime wedges to serve

AVOCADO DIP

1 avocado, mashed

125 ml full-cream Greek
**   yoghurt**

juice of 1 lime

salt and freshly ground black
**   pepper to taste**

1. To make the dip, combine all the ingredients and refrigerate until needed.
2. Bring a litre of water to the boil in a medium saucepan with a lid and cover with a vegetable steamer or colander.
3. Place the broccoli and asparagus in the steamer or colander, put on the lid and steam for 3–5 minutes until the vegetables are just tender.
4. Fill a bowl with cold water and ice cubes and transfer the vegetables straight from the steamer into the water to halt the cooking process.
5. Remove from the water and drain on a dry kitchen cloth.
6. Place the vegetables on a serving plate and season with salt and pepper.
7. Serve immediately with the avocado dip and fresh lime wedges.

Joy: The fullness of real joy can only be experienced if you have someone to share it with.

SALADS

We eat salad at least once a day. It is really worthwhile to grow your own salad leaves and varieties of tomatoes. The best part is that you can pick only what you need for the day. If you do not have a big garden, grow your salad ingredients in pots – as long as they have sunshine they will thrive. Salad leaves do not take up that much space, are easy to maintain and will usually keep for up to 14 days in a plastic bag in the fridge.

Mixed leaf
SALAD

SERVES 4–6 AS A SIDE SALAD

100 g mixed salad leaves
125 g rosa or cherry tomatoes
½ cucumber, sliced
olive oil and balsamic vinegar to drizzle
salt and freshly ground black pepper to taste

1. Place the salad leaves, tomatoes and cucumber in a salad bowl.
2. Drizzle over some olive oil and balsamic vinegar.
3. Season with salt and pepper to taste.
4. Lightly toss.

This is a very simple salad, but it complements any meaty pasta dish, such as lasagne or conchigliette with bolognaise.

Baby potato
SALAD

1 kg baby potatoes

salt and freshly ground black pepper to taste

250 ml salad cream

5 ml white sugar

45 ml plain yoghurt

3 spring onions, chopped

1. Boil the potatoes, skin on, in water in a medium saucepan until soft.
2. Remove the potatoes from the water and allow them to cool down completely.
3. Place them in a serving dish and season with salt and pepper.
4. Mix the salad cream, sugar and yoghurt, and pour over the potatoes. Toss gently to coat.
5. Garnish with the chopped spring onions.

Grilled steak and
CORN SALAD

4 x 200 g Scotch fillet or rib-eye steak

3 sweetcorn cobs

60 ml olive oil

salt to taste

250 ml fresh coriander

1 small red onion, sliced

200 g rosa tomatoes

60 ml lime juice

freshly ground black pepper to taste

DRESSING

30 ml olive oil

15 ml balsamic vinegar

15 ml chutney

1. Brush the steak and corn cobs with the olive oil.
2. Heat a griddle pan and char-grill the corn cobs on all sides. Set aside to cool slightly.
3. In the same pan, grill the steaks according to preference. Set aside on a cutting board to rest and season with salt.
4. Cut the kernels from the corn cobs and thinly slice the steaks.
5. Place the coriander, onion, tomatoes, steak and corn kernels in a salad bowl and gently toss.
6. Drizzle over the lime juice, and season with salt and pepper.
7. Mix the dressing ingredients and drizzle over the salad.

Mixed salad leaves can be substituted for the coriander.

Grilled baby marrow and
GREEN BEAN SALAD

50 g flaked almonds

15 ml olive oil

250 g French beans, topped and tailed

3 medium baby marrows

80 g mixed salad leaves

sea-salt flakes and freshly ground black pepper to taste

juice of 1 lime

1. Toast the flaked almonds in a dry frying pan over medium heat and set aside to cool.
2. Heat the olive oil in a large frying pan and fry the beans until bright green. Set aside to cool.
3. Using a vegetable peeler, thinly slice the baby marrows into long strips 1–2 mm thick.
4. Heat a griddle pan and grill the baby marrows until slightly charred. Set aside to cool.
5. Place the salad leaves in a shallow serving dish and top with the beans and baby marrow strips.
6. Sprinkle over the toasted flaked almonds and season with salt and pepper.
7. Dress with the lime juice.

Pea, broccoli, bacon and
AVOCADO SALAD

SERVES 6–8 AS A SIDE SALAD

150 g fresh tenderstem
    broccoli

250 ml frozen baby peas

15 ml olive oil

3–4 rashers bacon, diced

100 g mixed salad leaves

140 g sugar snap peas

1 avocado

juice of 1 lemon

salt and freshly ground black
    pepper to taste

30–40 ml smooth cottage
    cheese

DRESSING

15 ml balsamic vinegar

15 ml chutney

10 ml brown sugar

1. Cut the broccoli into smaller pieces if necessary.
2. Bring a medium saucepan of water to the boil and set a colander or strainer on top.
3. Add the broccoli to the colander, cover the saucepan with a lid, and steam the broccoli until it turns bright green.
4. Remove the broccoli and immediately submerge it in ice-cold water containing ice cubes to stop the cooking process. Once cooled, drain and dry the broccoli on paper towel.
5. Steam the frozen baby peas following the same procedure.
6. Heat the olive oil in a small frying pan over medium heat and fry the bacon until crispy. Drain off the fat and set aside to cool.
7. Place the salad leaves in a large serving bowl and top with the broccoli, sugar snap peas and baby peas.
8. Peel and slice the avocado into strips, drizzle with the lemon juice and add to the salad, along with the bacon.
9. Season with salt and pepper and add 6–8 teaspoon-sized dollops of cottage cheese.
10. Mix the dressing ingredients until the sugar has dissolved and drizzle over the salad.

Roasted butternut, beetroot and FETA SALAD

800 g butternut

15 ml olive oil

30 ml honey

salt to taste

100 g mixed salad leaves

400 g cooked fresh
   baby beetroot

120 g plain feta cheese, cubed

30 ml pumpkin seeds

freshly ground black pepper
   to taste

sweet balsamic vinegar
   to serve

1. Preheat the oven to 180 ˚C.
2. Cut the butternut into 1.5 cm thick discs and peel each disc. Cut into wedges.
3. Place the butternut in a single layer in a roasting dish and drizzle over the olive oil.
4. Bake for 30 minutes, turning once halfway through.
5. Remove from the oven, drizzle over the honey, season with salt and bake for another 5 minutes.
6. Remove from the oven and leave to cool.
7. Place the salad leaves and cooled butternut onto a large serving plate.
8. Cut the beetroot into halves or quarters and add to the salad.
9. Add the feta and sprinkle over the pumpkin seeds.
10. Season with salt and pepper to taste and serve with sweet balsamic vinegar on the side.

Strawberry, papaya and ROSA TOMATO SALAD

SERVES 8–10 AS A SIDE SALAD

100 g mixed salad leaves

1 medium papaya, cut into fingers

200 g rosa tomatoes, halved

200 g fresh strawberries, hulled and halved

1–2 discs plain feta cheese, cubed

salt and freshly ground black pepper to taste

creamy Caesar salad dressing to serve

1. Place the salad leaves onto a large serving plate and top with the papaya, tomatoes and strawberries.
2. Scatter over the feta and season with salt and pepper.
3. Serve with a creamy Caesar salad dressing.

Watercress and
BEETROOT SALAD

100 g watercress

80 g raw beetroot, peeled and julienned

80 g carrots, peeled and julienned

olive oil and balsamic vinegar to drizzle

salt and freshly ground black pepper to taste

1. Place the watercress onto a serving plate and add the beetroot and carrots.
2. Drizzle over some olive oil and balsamic vinegar and season with salt and pepper.
3. Lightly toss.

This salad is very light and is ideal to serve as a starter or side to rich, creamy, butter-based dishes.

Sweet chilli chicken and PINEAPPLE SALAD WITH CROUTONS

SERVES 4 AS A MAIN MEAL

15 ml olive oil

4 deboned skinless chicken
    breasts, cut into thin strips

150 ml sweet chilli sauce

5 ml salt

½ medium pineapple

180 g mixed salad leaves

10 cm cucumber, sliced

1 red pepper, deseeded
    and sliced

125 ml halved rosa or
    cherry tomatoes

80 g sugar snap peas

250 ml croutons

salt and freshly ground black
    pepper to taste

1. Heat the olive oil in a large frying pan over medium–high heat and fry the chicken strips until cooked.
2. Add the sweet chilli sauce and salt and fry for a further 2 minutes. Remove from the heat.
3. Peel the pineapple and cut it into 1 cm discs. Slice these into strips.
4. Place the salad leaves onto a large serving plate and add the cucumber, red pepper, tomatoes, sugar snap peas and pineapple.
5. Add the chicken strips and the croutons and lightly toss.
6. Season with salt and pepper to taste and serve immediately.

This makes a great light, yet filling, lunch.

Humility: Humility is the quality of courteously being respectful of others.

SOUPS

Steaming bowls of soup and fresh-baked bread are synonymous with cold winter evenings by the fireplace. When entertaining friends or family with a soup evening, I usually serve two to three different soups with a few different types of bread. Simple food, but truly hearty!

Biltong SOUP

15 ml olive oil

2 leeks, thinly sliced

4 medium potatoes, peeled and diced

750 ml water

10 ml chicken stock powder

60 g powdered biltong

salt and freshly ground black pepper to taste

125 ml cream

sliced biltong to serve

1. Heat the olive oil in a medium saucepan with a lid and sauté the leeks until softened.
2. Add the potatoes, water and stock powder, put on the lid and simmer for 20–30 minutes until the potatoes are soft.
3. Blend the soup until smooth, then return it to the stovetop and reheat.
4. Stir in the powdered biltong and season to taste.
5. Stir in the cream and serve hot, topped with slices of biltong.

Broccoli and blue cheese SOUP

SERVES 4–6

15 ml olive oil

1 leek, white part only, sliced

1 litre water

10 ml chicken stock powder

1 medium potato, peeled and diced

1 head broccoli, chopped

2 baby marrows, chopped

salt and freshly ground black pepper to taste

100 ml thin cream

75 g mild blue cheese, crumbled

a handful of watercress to garnish

1. Heat the olive oil in a medium saucepan with a lid over medium heat and sauté the leek until tender.
2. Add the water, stock powder and potato and bring to the boil. Reduce the heat, put on the lid and simmer for 20–30 minutes until the potato is cooked.
3. Add the broccoli and baby marrows and cook, covered, for a further 5 minutes until soft.
4. Purée the soup in a blender, then return it to the saucepan and reheat.
5. Season to taste and stir in the cream just before serving.
6. Serve hot, garnished with the crumbled blue cheese, extra black pepper and watercress.

Cream of tomato SOUP

SERVES 6–8

875 ml water

20 ml chicken stock powder

2 x 410 g cans tomato purée

10 ml salt

2.5 ml freshly ground black pepper

60 ml brown sugar

30 ml Worcestershire sauce

1.25 ml Tabasco® sauce

5 ml dried basil

125 ml cream

fresh basil leaves to garnish (optional)

1. Bring the water and stock powder to the boil in a large saucepan.
2. Add the tomato purée and stir.
3. Add the salt, pepper, sugar, Worcestershire sauce, Tabasco® sauce and basil.
4. Turn down the heat and simmer for 5 minutes.
5. Stir in the cream and simmer for a further 2 minutes.
6. Serve hot, garnished with fresh basil.

Some tomato purées are more tangy than others. Add more sugar if needed.

Pea and ham SOUP

15 ml butter

1 medium onion, diced

1 litre water

15 ml chicken stock powder

5 ml salt

1 medium potato, peeled and thinly sliced

500 g frozen young peas

200 g ham, cut into 1 cm cubes

1. Heat the butter in a large saucepan with a lid and gently sauté the onion until soft.
2. Add the water, stock powder and salt and bring to the boil.
3. Add the potato and frozen peas and bring to the boil once more.
4. Turn down the heat to medium and cook, covered, for 15–20 minutes until the potato is soft.
5. While the soup is cooking, heat a frying pan and gently fry the ham until crispy.
6. Purée the soup in a blender, pour into a clean saucepan and reheat.
7. Spoon the hot soup into bowls and garnish with the crispy ham.

Red bean SOUP

1 kg beef shin

7.5 ml salt

500 g dried red beans

4 stalks celery, finely chopped

2 leeks, finely chopped

2 large carrots, peeled
and grated

a bunch of fresh parsley,
finely chopped

20 ml beef stock powder

15 ml oil

250 g streaky bacon, diced

30 ml Worcestershire sauce

freshly ground black pepper
to taste

1. Place the beef in a slow cooker, adding 5 ml of the salt and enough water to cover. Cook on low overnight.
2. Soak the red beans overnight in a large bowl of cold water.
3. The following day, rinse the beans well and place them in a large saucepan with a lid. Cover with water, add the remaining salt and cook for 3–4 hours until soft. Drain and set aside.
4. Bring 2 litres water to the boil in a separate large saucepan with a lid.
5. Place all the vegetables, parsley and the stock powder into the boiling water and cook, covered, for 20–30 minutes until soft.
6. Add half of the beans to the cooked vegetables. Pour the soup in batches into a blender or food processor and purée, keeping it fairly chunky.
7. Heat the oil in a large clean saucepan and fry the bacon until just crispy. (Set some aside for garnishing later if desired.)
8. Add the remaining beans and the puréed soup to the bacon in the saucepan.
9. Remove the beef from the slow cooker, retaining the stock.
10. Take the meat off the bone and add to the soup.
11. Strain the beef stock through a sieve and add the strained liquid to the soup, 125 ml at a time, until it reaches a thick but pourable consistency.
12. Add the Worcestershire sauce and season with extra salt (if necessary) and pepper.
13. Reheat and serve hot, garnished with the reserved crispy bacon (optional).

This is my late grandmother Bessie Keulder's recipe. The tasty soup brings back fond memories of a big pot of steaming bean soup, warm bread and happy family visits.

Spicy butternut SOUP

SERVES 6

15 ml olive oil

1 leek, cut into 2 mm-thick slices

2.5–5 ml medium curry powder

5 ml ground cinnamon

1 litre water

10 ml chicken stock powder

1 kg butternut, peeled and cubed

7.5 ml salt

125 ml cream

1. Heat the olive oil in a large saucepan with a lid over medium heat and sauté the leek until soft.
2. Add the curry powder and cinnamon and sauté for 30 seconds.
3. Add the water, stock powder, butternut and salt, and bring to the boil.
4. Turn down the heat to medium, put on the lid and simmer for about 20 minutes until the butternut is soft.
5. Remove from the heat and allow to cool slightly before blending in batches in a blender or food processor until puréed and smooth.
6. Pour the soup into a clean saucepan and reheat.
7. Spoon into bowls, adding a swirl of cream to each.
8. Serve hot.

I love the light curry and cinnamon notes in this soup – they really bring a little extra warmth to the dish.

Baby marrow and feta
SOUP

SERVES 4

1.2 kg baby marrows, thinly sliced

2 turnips, peeled and grated

2 leeks, thinly sliced

750 ml water

15 ml chicken stock powder

5 ml salt

freshly ground black pepper to taste

125 ml cream

1 disc plain feta cheese, crumbled

a handful of watercress to garnish

1. Place all the vegetables in a large saucepan with a lid and add the water, stock powder and salt.
2. Put on the lid and cook over medium heat for 10–12 minutes until the vegetables are soft. Do not overcook, as the baby marrows will lose their green colour.
3. Pour the soup into a blender or food processor and blend until smooth.
4. Return the soup to the saucepan, reheat and season with pepper.
5. Serve in bowls garnished with a swirl of cream, crumbled feta and watercress.

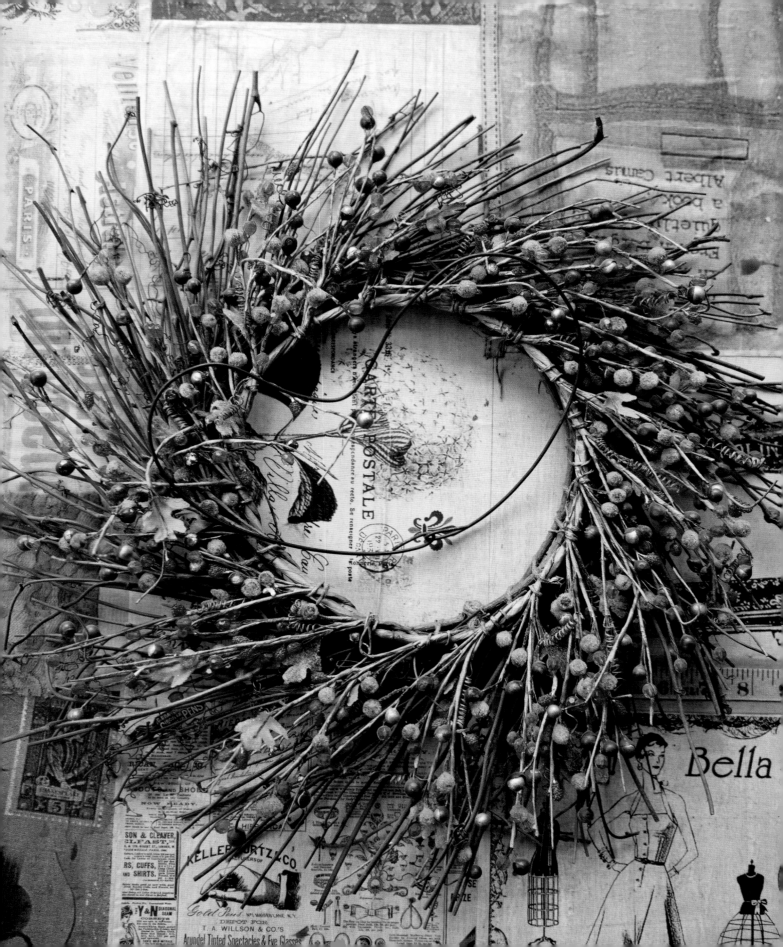

BREADS, PIZZAS AND QUICHES

Nothing smells more like home than fresh-baked bread. And nothing says 'family time' like a pizza evening. We usually start off with a focaccia as a starter. We then take turns in choosing the toppings and eat the pizzas as they come out of the oven. Depending on your appetite, you can bake and eat and have fun all night long! And when you feel like something lighter, what could be better than a quiche? Freshly baked quiche served with a side salad is one of my favourite lunches.

Farm-style BREAD

1 kg store-bought white
bread dough
butter and sliced biltong
to serve

1. Spray a 35 x 15 cm loaf tin with non-stick cooking spray.
2. Shape the dough with your hands to fit the tin.
3. Put the dough into the tin and cover with cling wrap and a clean cloth.
4. Let it prove in a warm place for 30–60 minutes until the dough has doubled in size – the pan must be just full.
5. When almost ready to bake, preheat the oven to 225 °C.
6. Remove the cling wrap and cloth and bake the bread for 35–40 minutes until cooked. It should sound hollow when tapped on the top.
7. Turn out onto a breadboard and leave to cool.
8. Slice and serve with butter and biltong, or your favourite topping.

My grandmother, Hetta du Bruyn, used to bake large farm-style loaves in her AGA coal stove. This is a tribute to her bread. It is best enjoyed once cooled on the day of baking, with butter and some sliced biltong. You don't have to make your own dough; you can buy fresh dough from your local bakery.

Mini
BREAD ROLLS

1 kg store-bought white bread dough

125 ml cake flour

1. Grease with a little butter and then flour a baking tray.
2. Pinch off golf-ball sized amounts of the dough and roll into balls.
3. Place the dough balls 5–7 cm apart on the baking tray and sift over the flour.
4. Lightly cover with cling wrap and a clean cloth and leave to prove in a warm place for 20–30 minutes until nearly doubled in size.
5. When almost ready to bake, preheat the oven to 180 ˚C.
6. Remove the cling wrap and cloth and bake the rolls on the middle rack of the oven for 12–15 minutes until golden brown.
7. Serve warm with butter.

Mini
POT BREADS

MAKES 18 MINI POT BREADS

50 g butter
18 mini clay pots (6 x 6.5 cm)
1 kg store-bought white bread dough

1. Use the butter to grease the clay pots very well on the inside and outer edges.
2. Break off bits of dough and roll into balls just big enough to fill half a pot.
3. Place a dough ball inside each pot, cover with cling wrap or a dough cloth and leave to prove in a warm place for about 30 minutes until doubled in size.
4. When almost ready to bake, preheat the oven to 180 ˚C.
5. Remove the cling wrap or cloth and place all the clay pots in a 4–5 cm deep oven tray.
6. Carefully pour hot water into the tray until half full, creating a bain-marie.
7. Place the tray in the oven and bake for 20 minutes.

These mini pot breads will certainly impress when everybody gets their own individual little bread. Serve the pot breads warm with butter and sundried tomato pesto (see page 303).

ROOSTERKOEK

1 kg store-bought fresh white bread dough

extra flour to dust

1. Place the dough on a floured breadboard and slightly flatten it with your hands to about 4 cm thick.
2. Cut the dough into 3 cm wide strips and cut each strip into 3 x 3 cm squares.
3. Flatten each square with your fingertips to about 2 cm thick and 4–5 cm wide.
4. Flour a large baking tray and place the pieces of dough on the tray, about 4 cm apart.
5. Sprinkle with flour, cover the tray with cling wrap and a cloth and leave to prove in a warm place for 30–40 minutes until doubled in size.
6. When making these on the stovetop, spray a griddle pan with non-stick cooking spray.
7. Heat the pan over medium heat, add the pieces of dough, then reduce the heat and cook over low heat for 5–8 minutes per side until cooked through on all sides.
8. Serve the roosterkoek warm with butter and jam or honey.

Directly translated, roosterkoek means 'grill cake'. These small breads are usually cooked on a grid over a fire. You want the coals slightly cooler than for cooking meat. Spray the grid beforehand with non-stick cooking spray and position it as far away from the fire as possible. Keep turning until the dough is cooked through.

Chicken mayonnaise
TRAMEZZINI

SERVES 6

1 kg store-bought white
    bread dough
15 ml olive oil
6 skinless deboned
    chicken breasts
salt to taste
125–250 ml creamy
    mayonnaise
about 600 g mozzarella
    cheese, grated

1. Flour a large breadboard and divide the dough into six parts. Form into balls and let them rest in a warm place, covered with floured cling wrap, until doubled in size.
2. On a well-floured surface, roll out each ball to form a 16 cm disc.
3. Heat a dry frying pan over low heat and grill each dough disc for 3–4 minutes on each side until cooked.
4. Tip onto a cooling rack and repeat until all the tramezzini breads are cooked.
5. Heat the olive oil over medium heat in a separate large frying pan.
6. Flatten the chicken breasts to 1 cm thick and season with salt.
7. Lightly fry the chicken breasts until just cooked. Remove from the pan, slice finely and allow to cool slightly.
8. Combine the chicken with enough mayonnaise to coat well and divide into six portions.
9. Preheat a sandwich press.
10. Cut the tramezzini breads horizontally, as you would a bread roll.
11. Fill each with chicken mayonnaise, topped with 100 g grated mozzarella. Place on the sandwich press.
12. Close the press and toast for a few minutes until the mozzarella has melted.
13. Keep the tramezzinis warm while you toast the rest.
14. Cut into quarters and serve warm with a side salad.

You will need a sandwich press to make the tramezzini. Although homemade tramezzinis need a little more effort, they definitely taste better than store-bought.

Italian-style
BAGUETTE

5 ml olive oil

150 g Eureka stoneground
cake flour

250 g Eureka stoneground
white bread flour

10 g instant dry yeast

5 ml salt

400 ml lukewarm water

1. Brush the bowl of an electric mixer with the olive oil and add the flours and yeast. Attach the dough hook.
2. Stir the salt into 100 ml of the water and set aside.
3. Turn the mixer onto low speed, add the remaining 300 ml water to the flour and mix.
4. Add the salt water and knead for 5–8 minutes, until the dough comes away from the sides of the bowl.
5. Cover the bowl with cling wrap and a cloth and leave the dough to prove in a warm place for 30–60 minutes until doubled in size.
6. When almost ready to bake, preheat the oven to 200 ˚C and place a baking tray or pizza tile inside to heat up.
7. Turn out the dough onto a well-floured surface, divide in half and form two balls.
8. Roll each ball into a long thin sausage with pointed ends.
9. With a sharp knife, make three thin diagonal cuts, 3 mm deep, in each roll (be careful not to cut all the way through).
10. Flour the preheated baking tray or pizza tile and place the breads onto it, 10 cm apart.
11. Bake for 35 minutes.
12. Cool on a wooden breadboard before slicing at a slight angle to serve.

This baguette is so versatile that it complements any meal. You can even serve it as a starter with condiments such as pesto, olive oil and balsamic vinegar.

Ciabatta BREAD

MAKES 1 LOAF

400 g Eureka unbleached
    stoneground cake flour
340 ml (325 g) water at
    room temperature
5 ml instant dry yeast
5 ml salt
15 ml olive oil

1. Heap the flour on a clean surface and make a well in the middle.*
2. For greater accuracy, measure out the water by weight and then stir in the yeast.
3. Pour three-quarters of the water a little at a time into the well in the flour and mix with your hands after each addition.
4. Stir the salt into the last quarter of water and add this to the flour.
5. Knead for 15–20 minutes to form an elastic, soft, shiny and sticky dough. (Do not add any extra flour!)
6. Oil a large mixing bowl with the olive oil. Place the dough in the bowl, cover with cling wrap and a cloth and leave to rest at room temperature for 12 hours.
7. Once the dough has rested, flour your work surface very well. Then flour a proving cloth (thick unbleached linen works well) and place it on a breadboard.
8. Wet your hands and gently scrape the dough from the bowl onto the floured work surface (do not let it drop). You want to keep as much air in the dough as possible.
9. Gently lift the dough by putting your hands underneath it and start stretching it into a rectangle 30–40 cm long and 15 cm wide. Gently place the stretched dough back onto the flour.

Artisan bread is bread at its best. 'Artisan' is the term used to describe bread that is handcrafted with local unbleached, stoneground flour in a careful process. Ciabatta or slipper bread has a crunchy and chewy crust and distinct holes that develop over hours of slow proving so that the dough becomes a sourdough. Make the dough early in the morning to have bread for the evening, or in the evening to have it ready by lunchtime the next day. Although the proving time is long, the process is simple. And the longer the proving, the less yeast you will need. If you really want good bread, be patient! This ciabatta makes delicious sandwiches and can be served with any meal.

10. Fold the left side to the middle, then fold the right side over the left. Pick up the dough with both hands at the open ends and stretch to about 25 cm long.

11. Place immediately on the floured proving cloth, folded side of the dough up. Fold in the sides of the cloth so that they stand up to support the sides of the bread. Dust flour over the dough, cover with cling wrap and a clean cloth and prove in a warm place until nearly doubled in size (45–60 minutes in summer and 1–2 hours in winter).

12. In the meantime, place a pizza tile or baking tray in the oven and preheat to 225 °C.

13. When the dough is ready, remove the tile or tray from the oven and lightly flour it.

14. Remove the cloth and cling wrap from the dough and gently roll it from the proving cloth, folded side down, onto the pizza tile or tray without knocking out air. The dough will look flat, but will rise in the oven.

15. Place the bread on the middle rack of the oven, throw one ice cube onto the bottom of the oven to make steam and immediately close the door. Bake for 35 minutes until medium brown.

16. Tap the bread with your finger. It will sound hollow if done.

17. Cool on a wooden board before cutting with a sharp bread knife. The crust should be crispy and chewy, and the inside soft.

* You can also make the dough with an electric mixer, using the dough hook. Grease the bowl with olive oil and add the flour. Stir the yeast into the water. With the mixer running on low speed, slowly add three-quarters of the water to the flour. Stir the salt into the remaining quarter of water and add this to the flour. Knead on medium–high speed for 5–8 minutes until all the dough comes away from the sides of the bowl and is shiny, soft, sticky and elastic. Cover the bowl with cling wrap and a cloth and leave to rest at room temperature for 12 hours.

Steamed MEALIE BREAD

butter to grease

10–12 fresh white mealies

30 g butter, melted

125 ml cream

6 eggs, beaten

250–375 ml cake flour, sifted

25 ml baking powder

15 ml white sugar

10 ml salt

1. You will need two round tins, about 11 cm in diameter and 13 cm high, with tight-fitting lids. Grease the tins and the inside of their lids with butter. Line the lids and tins, bottoms and sides, with foil. Butter the lined tins and lids again, over the foil.

2. Clean the mealies by removing all the leaves and hair, then cut the corn from the cobs. You will need 1.6 litres of corn.

3. Mince the corn in a food processor or with a mincer and tip into a large bowl.

4. Add the melted butter, cream and beaten eggs, and mix well.

5. Add 250 ml flour, the baking powder, sugar and salt. Mix to a thick but pourable consistency. If the mixture is too runny, add more flour.

6. Pour the mixture into the two tins, filling until three-quarters full, and cover with the lids.

7. Fill one large or two smaller saucepans (with tight-fitting lids) large enough to accommodate the tins with enough water to cover three-quarters of the tins when submerged. Bring to the boil.

8. Carefully lower the tins into the water and cover the saucepan/s.

9. Steam the breads over medium heat for 2 hours. Keep topping up the saucepan/s with hot water throughout the cooking time.

10. Remove the tins and allow to cool slightly before opening and gently turning out the breads onto a breadboard. Cool just enough to unwrap the foil, then slice into discs with an electric knife and serve warm with butter.

Mealie bread is probably better known on the maize farms in the Free State. We usually make this bread from December to February when fresh white mealies (also called green mealies) are readily available. They are usually sold at farmstalls or at the side of the road and can be kept for up to four days in the fridge before being used in this bread. We prefer having mealie bread as a starch with a braai and salad.

Health BREAD

500 g brown bread flour

5 ml salt

10 g instant dry yeast

250 ml muesli with nuts
   and raisins

125 ml raisins

125 ml sunflower seeds

60 ml linseeds

60 ml sesame seeds

500 ml lukewarm water

15 ml honey

45 ml poppy seeds

1. Combine all the ingredients up to and including the sesame seeds in the bowl of an electric mixer.
2. Add the water and honey.
3. Knead with a dough hook on medium speed for about 5 minutes until the dough comes away from the sides of the bowl.
4. Spray a 30 x 10 cm loaf tin with non-stick cooking spray.
5. Gently press the dough into the tin, cover with cling wrap and a cloth and leave to prove in a warm place for 30–40 minutes until the dough has risen. It should be rounded and fill the tin (don't let it rise over the tin or over-prove, otherwise it will collapse).
6. When almost ready to bake, preheat the oven to 200 ˚C.
7. Sprinkle the poppy seeds over the top of the bread and bake for 35 minutes until a skewer inserted into the centre comes out clean.
8. Turn out onto a breadboard and allow to cool completely before slicing and serving.

We used to buy bread similar to this one on the South Coast, but it was often difficult to find and not available everywhere, so I decided to make my own. This bread is not only delicious freshly baked, but also makes beautiful toast the next day, and the next ...

Almond and cinnamon BREAD

**1 kg store-bought white
    bread dough**
50 ml soft butter
150 ml brown sugar
20 ml ground cinnamon
100 g flaked almonds
250–280 ml icing sugar
30 ml water
2.5 ml vanilla essence

1. Line a large baking tray with baking paper and spray with non-stick cooking spray.
2. Dust your work surface and rolling pin with flour and roll out the dough into a rectangle of approximately 40 x 50 cm.
3. Using a palette knife, spread the butter over the entire rectangle of dough.
4. Sprinkle with the brown sugar and then the cinnamon.
5. Starting at the long side of the rectangle, roll the dough into a long roll and transfer it onto the baking tray.
6. Starting 2 cm from one end, cut the roll in half lengthways, right through to the end. The dough will fold open.
7. Starting from the top, where the dough is still joined, plait the halves and fold and press the ends together.
8. Cover the tray with cling wrap and a cloth and leave the loaf to rise in a warm place for 1–2 hours until doubled in size.
9. When almost ready to bake, preheat the oven to 180 ˚C.
10. Sprinkle the risen dough with the flaked almonds and lightly cover with foil.
11. Bake for 45 minutes, then remove the foil and bake for another 15 minutes.
12. Mix 250 ml icing sugar with the water and vanilla essence. If it is too runny, add an extra 15–30 ml icing sugar to make a paste that just drips off the spoon.
13. Remove the bread from the oven and, starting at one end and using a twirling motion, drip the icing over the bread until most of it is covered. Leave to cool.
14. Slice into 1 cm thick slices and serve with lashings of butter.

This beautiful plaited bread has become a firm favourite whenever we entertain family or friends. I bake it in a 90 cm oven, but if your oven is smaller you can make two shorter loaves or form the plait into a circle.

Banana BREAD

MAKES 1 LOAF

125 g butter

180 ml white sugar

2 extra-large eggs

500 ml cake flour

10 ml baking powder

2.5 ml salt

5 ml vanilla essence

6 medium bananas, mashed

1. Preheat the oven to 180 °C and spray a 10 x 30 cm loaf tin with non-stick cooking spray.
2. Using an electric mixer, cream the butter and sugar until pale.
3. Keeping the mixer running, add the eggs, one at a time.
4. In a separate bowl, sift together the flour, baking powder and salt.
5. Add the dry ingredients to the egg mixture in four batches.
6. Add the vanilla essence and then mix in the mashed banana.
7. Pour the batter into the loaf tin and bake for 1 hour or until a skewer inserted into the centre comes out clean.
8. Turn out onto a breadboard and leave to cool before slicing and serving with lashings of butter.
9. Cover with foil and store in an airtight container. Use within four days.

This recipe is from my mother Marita Prinsloo's kitchen. She often packed it into our school lunchboxes. It is a delicious teatime treat and freezes well.

Italian
FOCACCIA

MAKES 5–6 FOCACCIA

7.5 ml salt

14 g instant dry yeast

2.5 ml white sugar

60 ml olive oil

50 ml milk

400 ml lukewarm water

700 g white bread flour

5 ml olive oil, plus extra
to drizzle

chopped fresh rosemary
to taste

chopped fresh garlic to taste

coarse sea salt to taste

1. Mix the salt, yeast, sugar, olive oil, milk and water.
2. Tip the flour onto a clean surface and make a well in the middle.*
3. Add the liquid in parts, mixing with your hands after every addition.
4. Once all the liquid has been added, knead the dough for 10–12 minutes until soft and elastic.
5. Oil a bowl with the olive oil and place the dough inside. Cover with cling wrap and leave the dough to prove for 15 minutes.
6. Place the dough on a well-floured breadboard and divide it into five or six equal pieces.
7. Form these into balls and place them on the board a few centimetres apart. Sprinkle with flour and cover with cling wrap and a cloth. Allow to prove in a warm place for 20–30 minutes until doubled in size.
8. Preheat the oven to 245 ˚C, bottom heat only, and place a pizza tile on the lowest rack.
9. Roll out a ball of dough into a thin circle, 2–3 mm thick.
10. Flour the hot pizza tile, place the dough on the tile and sprinkle over chopped fresh rosemary and garlic.
11. Bake for 8–10 minutes. The dough might rise into a large bubble – this is fine.
12. Remove from the oven, drizzle over olive oil and sprinkle with salt.
13. Serve immediately while you bake the remaining focaccia.

* When using an electric mixer, place the flour and yeast in the bowl. Pour in the liquid and, using a dough hook, mix on low speed. Knead at medium speed for 5–8 minutes until the dough comes away from the sides of the bowl. Cover with cling wrap and leave to prove for 15 minutes.

When we as a family make pizzas at home, we usually make a focaccia as a starter. If you only want to make one or two focaccia, use the rest of the dough for pizza bases.

Basic Italian
PIZZA BASE

700 g white bread flour

14 g active dry yeast

60 ml olive oil

50 ml milk

7.5 ml salt

2.5 ml white sugar

400 ml lukewarm water

1. Place the flour in the bowl of an electric mixer with a dough hook.*
2. Mix the yeast, olive oil, milk, salt and sugar into the water.
3. Slowly add the liquid to the flour while mixing on low speed, then knead on medium speed for 5–8 minutes until the dough comes away from the sides of the bowl.
4. Cover with cling wrap and rest the dough for 15 minutes.
5. Place the dough on a well-floured breadboard and divide into six equal portions.
6. Form each portion into a ball and place them on the board a few centimetres apart.
7. Cover the board with cling wrap and a cloth and rest in a warm place for 20–30 minutes until the dough has doubled in size.
8. Preheat the oven to 245 °C and place a pizza tile or baking tray on the lowest rack.
9. On a well-floured surface, roll a ball of dough into a thin circle, about 30 cm in diameter and 2–3 mm thick.
10. Lightly flour the hot tile or tray and place the pizza base on top.
11. Quickly add your choice of toppings and bake on the lowest oven rack for 8–10 minutes until any cheese you have added has melted and the edges of the base are golden and crispy.

* To make the dough by hand, heap the flour on a clean surface and make a well in the middle. Add the liquid in parts, mixing after every addition. Knead for 10–12 minutes until soft and elastic. Rest in an oiled bowl covered with cling wrap for 15 minutes.

STEAK AND ONION PIZZA
with rocket

1 basic Italian pizza base (see page 92)

1 portion tomato base for pizza (see page 309)

15 ml butter

1 onion, sliced into rings

250 g brown mushrooms, sliced

100 g beef steak

15 ml olive oil

salt and freshly ground black pepper to taste

250 ml grated mozzarella cheese

100 g fresh rocket leaves

1. Prepare your pizza base and tomato base in advance.
2. Preheat the oven to 245 °C and place a pizza tile or baking tray on the lowest rack.
3. Heat the butter in a small frying pan and slowly sauté the onion until soft. Set aside.
4. In the same pan, sauté the mushrooms until softened. Set aside.
5. Heat a griddle pan and brush the steak with the olive oil.
6. Grill the steak on both sides until cooked to medium, then remove from the heat and rest for 5 minutes. Season and slice into thin strips.
7. Lightly flour the hot pizza tile or baking tray and place the pizza base on top.
8. Working quickly, spread the tomato base over the pizza base and sprinkle with the grated cheese. Add the onion, followed by the mushrooms and finally the beef strips.
9. Bake on the lowest oven rack for 8–10 minutes until the cheese has melted.
10. Garnish with the fresh rocket and some black pepper, slide onto a pizza board and serve immediately.

HONEY-GLAZED CHICKEN AND AVOCADO PIZZA
with cherry tomatoes

MAKES 1 LARGE PIZZA

1 basic Italian pizza base (see page 92)

1 portion tomato base for pizza (see page 309)

100 g deboned chicken breast

15 ml olive oil

30–45 ml honey

salt and freshly ground black pepper to taste

250 ml grated mozzarella cheese

10 cherry tomatoes, halved

1 avocado, sliced

a small handful of fresh rocket leaves

1. Prepare your pizza base and tomato base in advance.
2. Preheat the oven to 245 °C and place a pizza tile or baking tray on the lowest rack.
3. Beat the chicken breast with a meat mallet to 1 cm thick and cut into thin strips.
4. Heat the olive oil in a frying pan over medium heat and fry the chicken strips until cooked. Add the honey to taste, season and fry for another minute.
5. Lightly flour the hot pizza tile or baking tray and place the pizza base on top.
6. Working quickly, spread the tomato base over the pizza base and sprinkle with the grated cheese. Add the chicken strips, followed by the cherry tomatoes.
7. Bake on the lowest oven rack for 8–10 minutes until the cheese has melted.
8. Garnish with avocado slices, fresh rocket and some black pepper, slide onto a pizza board and serve immediately.

FRENCH
WINE BARREL

Spinach, bacon and feta PIZZA

1 basic Italian pizza base (see page 92)

30 ml olive oil

150 g baby spinach leaves

salt and freshly ground black pepper to taste

150 g rindless bacon, cut into small pieces

250 ml grated mozzarella cheese

1 disc plain feta cheese

1. Prepare your pizza base in advance.
2. Preheat the oven to 245 °C and place a pizza tile or baking tray on the lowest rack.
3. Heat a frying pan over medium heat, add 15 ml of the olive oil and cook the spinach leaves until they change colour to bright green. Season and set aside.
4. Heat the remaining olive oil in the same pan and fry the bacon until cooked.
5. Lightly flour the hot pizza tile or baking tray and place the pizza base on top.
6. Sprinkle the grated cheese over the pizza base and top with the spinach, followed by the bacon.
7. Bake on the lowest oven rack for 8–10 minutes until the mozzarella has melted.
8. Crumble over the feta, season with black pepper, slide onto a pizza board and serve immediately.

SALAMI AND MUSHROOM PIZZA
with buffalo mozzarella

MAKES 1 LARGE PIZZA

1 basic Italian pizza base (see
    page 92)
15 ml butter
250 g brown mushrooms,
    sliced
salt and freshly ground black
    pepper to taste
250 ml grated mozzarella
    cheese
100 g salami, sliced
6–8 buffalo mozzarella balls
truffle oil to drizzle
100 g fresh basil leaves

1. Prepare your pizza base in advance.
2. Preheat the oven to 245 ˚C and place a pizza tile or baking tray on the lowest rack.
3. Heat the butter in a frying pan and slowly sauté the mushrooms until softened. Season to taste.
4. Lightly flour the hot pizza tile or baking tray and place the pizza base on top.
5. Sprinkle the grated cheese over the pizza base and top with the mushrooms and salami.
6. Tear half of the buffalo mozzarella balls in half and place them on the pizza.
7. Bake on the lowest oven rack for 8–10 minutes until the cheese has melted.
8. Tear the remaining buffalo mozzarella balls into quarters and scatter them over the cooked pizza.
9. Lightly drizzle the pizza with truffle oil, season with black pepper and garnish with fresh basil leaves.
10. Slide onto a pizza board and serve immediately.

If you can find truffle oil, it is really worth trying on this pizza. It adds a wonderful, delectable truffle/mushroom flavour.

Cherry tomato QUICHE

PASTRY

250 ml cake flour, sifted

150 g cold butter, cut into
    1 cm cubes

250 ml grated Cheddar cheese

FILLING

30 ml butter

1 onion, diced

300 g cherry tomatoes, halved

4 egg yolks

250 ml cream

salt and freshly ground black
    pepper to taste

125 ml grated Cheddar cheese

fresh basil leaves to garnish

1. Grease a 26 cm quiche tin.
2. To make the pastry, place the flour in a mixing bowl, add the butter and mix with an electric mixer or by hand until it resembles coarse crumbs.
3. Add the grated cheese and mix until it comes together in a soft dough.
4. Gently form the dough into a ball and press flat to about 2 cm thick.
5. Cover the dough with cling wrap and rest it in the fridge for 20 minutes.
6. Using a rolling pin, roll out the dough on a well-floured surface into a circle 3–4 cm bigger than the quiche tin.
7. Roll the pastry gently over the rolling pin and unroll it over the quiche tin. Press the pastry into the bottom and sides and trim off any excess.
8. Preheat the oven to 180 ˚C and prepare the filling as follows.
9. Heat the butter in a frying pan over medium heat and sauté the onion until soft.
10. Spread the onion over the pastry base and pack the tomato halves on top, cut-side up, until the base is covered.
11. Beat the egg yolks in a small bowl, add the cream and mix well.
12. Pour the egg mixture over the tomatoes, covering the whole quiche.
13. Season with salt and pepper and sprinkle over the grated cheese.
14. Bake for 30–35 minutes, until the custard has set.
15. Rest the quiche for at least 10 minutes before serving garnished with fresh basil.

When I make quiche, I use the leftover egg whites to make meringues.

Spinach and feta
QUICHE

PASTRY

250 ml cake flour, sifted

150 g cold butter, cut into
    1 cm cubes

250 ml grated Cheddar cheese

FILLING

30 ml butter

1 onion, diced

150–200 g baby spinach leaves

125 g plain feta cheese,
    crumbled

4 egg yolks

250 ml cream

salt and freshly ground black
    pepper to taste

125 ml grated Cheddar cheese

1. Grease six 12 cm quiche dishes (or a 26 cm quiche tin for one large quiche) with a little butter.
2. To make the pastry, place the flour in a mixing bowl, add the butter and mix with an electric mixer or by hand until it resembles coarse crumbs.
3. Add the grated cheese and mix until it comes together into a soft dough.
4. Gently form the dough into a ball and press flat to about 2 cm thick.
5. Cover the dough with cling wrap and rest it in the fridge for 20 minutes.
6. Divide the dough into six equal portions. Using a rolling pin, roll out each portion on a well-floured surface into a circle 3–4 cm bigger than a quiche dish.
7. Roll the pastry gently over the rolling pin and unroll it over a quiche dish. Press the pastry to the bottom and sides and trim off any excess. Repeat with the remaining portions of dough.
8. Preheat the oven to 180 °C and prepare the filling as follows.
9. Heat the butter in a frying pan over medium heat and sauté the onion until soft.
10. Divide and spread the onion over the pastry bases.
11. Sauté the spinach in the same pan for 1–2 minutes until it changes colour to bright green. Divide and spread the spinach over the onion and then cover with crumbled feta.
12. Beat the egg yolks in a small bowl, add the cream and mix well.
13. Pour the egg mixture over the spinach until each quiche is covered.
14. Season with salt and pepper and sprinkle over the grated cheese.
15. Bake the quiches for 30–35 minutes until the custard is set.
16. Rest the quiches for at least 10 minutes before serving.

These are creamy and light, and perfect for a picnic.

Live life to the fullest: You only have today – yesterday is gone and tomorrow is unknown, so embrace today and make the best of it.

Live well laugh often love much.

PASTAS

Pasta-making is one of Italy's oldest traditions. It may seem like a daunting task, but once you've mastered it, you'll see how quick and easy it is and you will never buy readymade pasta again. Invest in a pasta machine and you are set for life. It's also a wonderful tool to involve the whole family in cooking. Pasta-making is such a fun way of bringing family or friends together and will guarantee unforgettable, tasty meals! Our youngest son Lou loves to make up his own pasta recipes and then calls them 'Pasta à la Lou'. So come on, I dare you to make 'Pasta à la You'! Grow fresh origanum, thyme and basil in your garden or in pots, as they are essential in Italian cooking.

Homemade
PASTA

1 litre cake flour

4 extra-large eggs

15–30 ml cold water

1. Sift the flour onto a clean work surface and make a well in the middle.
2. Break the eggs into the well and gradually mix in the flour until the mixture resembles breadcrumbs.
3. Add 15–30 ml water to make a firm but not sticky dough and knead until it becomes soft and pliable. Add more water if necessary.
4. Cover the dough with cling wrap and rest it for at least 90 minutes.
5. After it has rested, flatten the dough with the palm of your hand into a rectangle about 2 cm thick and 5 cm wide.
6. Set your pasta machine rollers to the widest setting and roll the dough through the machine, keeping it in a long strip.
7. Keep rolling the pasta dough through the machine using a smaller setting each time until the dough is 1–2 mm thick. If necessary, cut the pasta lengths in half to make them more manageable. Lay the rolled sheet(s) flat and cover with a wet cloth.
8. For lasagne, cut the pasta sheet into 10 x 15 cm rectangles and place them on a floured surface, uncovered and not touching or overlapping. Leave the pasta to dry – it should dry within 10–20 minutes.
9. For tagliatelle, fettuccini or spaghetti, cut the sheet into 20 cm lengths. Fix the required cutter to the machine and feed each strip through the cutter, catching the pasta on the other side with one hand. Hang each handful of pasta over a pasta drying rack. Separate the strands and lightly dust with flour. Allow the pasta to dry for at least half an hour.
10. When you are ready to cook your fettuccini or spaghetti, bring a large saucepan of water to the boil. Add 5 ml salt and cook the pasta in the boiling water for 5–10 minutes until al dente.
11. Drain and serve immediately with your favourite sauce.

Freshly made pasta cooks faster than store-bought pasta. Use 250 ml flour and 1 egg per person for a large serving. Make your pasta sauce while your pasta hangs on the drying rack. This ensures that when your pasta is cooked, you'll have a readymade sauce to serve immediately.

BUTTERNUT GNOCCHI
with Napoletana sauce

SERVES 4–6

500 g butternut, peeled
and diced
1 extra-large egg, beaten
250 ml cake flour, sifted
5 ml salt
60–90 ml finely grated
Parmesan cheese

NAPOLETANA SAUCE
15 ml olive oil
1 onion, diced
10 ml crushed garlic
2 x 410 g cans chopped
peeled tomatoes
30 ml tomato paste
15 ml dried Italian herbs
15 ml brown sugar
5 ml salt
freshly ground black pepper
to taste
fresh thyme to garnish

1. Place the butternut into a large saucepan and cover with a lid. Do not add water. Heat until the butternut starts to cook, turn down the heat and simmer until soft.
2. Allow the butternut to cool and then mash or purée in a food processor.
3. Place the butternut in a medium mixing bowl and stir in the beaten egg, followed by the flour, being careful not to overmix.
4. Cover the bowl with cling wrap and refrigerate for at least 90 minutes.
5. In the meantime, make the Napoletana sauce. Heat the oil in a medium saucepan and sauté the onion. Add the garlic and sauté for 1 minute, then add the tomatoes and bring to the boil.
6. Mix in the tomato paste, herbs, sugar and salt. Cook over low heat until reduced. Season to taste with black pepper and keep warm.
7. Place the butternut mixture onto a floured surface and roll it into long sausages 1.5 cm thick. Cut the sausages into small pillows.
8. Using a fork, lightly press down on each pillow and gently pull the fork towards you to create a classic gnocchi shape. Place the gnocchi on a floured breadboard while you cut and shape the rest.
9. In the meantime, half-fill a large saucepan with water and bring to the boil, adding the 5 ml salt.
10. Lift the breadboard over the boiling water and gently push some gnocchi into the water. Don't overcrowd; rather cook in batches.
11. The gnocchi are cooked when they rise to the surface of the water.
12. Spoon out the gnocchi with a slotted spoon and keep warm in a serving dish while you cook the rest.
13. Stir through the hot Napoletana sauce and serve garnished with the grated Parmesan and some fresh thyme.

If you have never had homemade gnocchi, you should definitely try this. It is so soft and tender that it melts in your mouth. This recipe provides a wonderful balance between the sweetness of the butternut gnocchi and the tanginess of the tomato base.

CLASSIC LASAGNE

SERVES 4–6

30 ml olive oil

1 onion, chopped

2–3 cloves garlic, chopped

500 g beef mince

5 ml salt

freshly ground black pepper
   to taste

410 g can chopped peeled
   tomatoes

50 g tomato paste

10 ml dried Italian herbs

5 ml brown sugar

125 ml water

9 homemade lasagne sheets
   (see page 108)

250 ml grated Parmesan
   cheese

500 ml grated mozzarella
   cheese

a handful of baby salad leaves
   to garnish

BÉCHAMEL SAUCE

1.25 litres full-cream milk

1 onion, roughly chopped

1 carrot, peeled and roughly
   chopped

1 bay leaf

100 g butter

250 ml cake flour

5 ml salt

freshly ground black pepper
   to taste

1. Preheat the oven to 180 °C and grease a 20 x 30 cm rectangular oven dish.
2. Heat the oil in a medium saucepan and sauté the onion until soft.
3. Add the garlic and cook for 2 minutes. Add the mince and fry over high heat, stirring continuously, for 5–10 minutes until cooked and loose.
4. Season with the salt and pepper to taste and add the tomatoes, tomato paste, herbs, sugar and water.
5. Put on the lid and cook over low heat for 15 minutes, always ensuring there is enough liquid and topping up with a bit of water if not.
6. In the meantime, make the béchamel sauce. Heat the milk, onion, carrot and bay leaf in a saucepan and simmer over low heat for 2 minutes. Strain and keep aside the milk, discarding the rest.
7. In a separate saucepan, melt the butter over medium heat and then add the flour and whisk for about 1 minute until smooth, forming a roux.
8. Gradually add the heated infused milk, 250 ml at a time, stirring constantly to prevent lumps from forming. Cook until the roux is smooth after every addition.
9. Simmer and stir over low heat for about 10 minutes until the sauce is thick, smooth and creamy. Add the salt and pepper to taste.
10. Starting with the pasta, layer three lasagne sheets in the base of the greased dish. Evenly spread over half of the bolognaise mince, followed by 250 ml béchamel sauce.
11. Sprinkle a third of the Parmesan cheese over the sauce, followed by a third of the mozzarella.
12. Repeat the layers and then top with one last layer of lasagne. Cover with 250 ml béchamel sauce. Sprinkle over the remaining cheeses.
13. Drizzle the remaining béchamel sauce on top and bake for 25–30 minutes until golden brown and cooked through.
14. Garnish with some baby salad leaves.

The meat sauce cooks the pasta so make sure the bolognaise mince does not cook dry. Serve with a mixed leaf salad (see page 46). This recipe can be doubled to serve 8–10 people. When doubling, use a 25 x 30–40 cm dish and four sheets of lasagne per layer instead of three (12 sheets).

CONCHIGLIETTE
with bolognaise and cheese sauce

SERVES 4–6

15 ml olive oil

1 onion, chopped

4 cloves garlic, chopped

500 g beef mince

410 g can chopped peeled
   tomatoes

50 g tomato paste

1 large carrot, peeled and
   coarsely grated

5 ml brown sugar

10 ml salt

freshly ground black pepper
   to taste

15 ml dried Italian herbs

2 litres water

500 g conchigliette
   (small pasta shells)

fresh origanum to garnish

CHEESE SAUCE

100 g butter

200 ml cake flour

1 litre full-cream milk

125 ml grated Parmesan or
   Cheddar cheese

2.5 ml salt

freshly ground black pepper
   to taste

1. Heat the oil over medium heat in a medium saucepan with a lid and sauté the onion and garlic until soft.
2. Add the mince and fry over high heat, stirring continuously, for 5–10 minutes until cooked and loose.
3. Add the tomatoes, tomato paste, carrot, sugar, half the salt and pepper to taste.
4. Put on the lid and simmer over low heat for 10 minutes until reduced.
5. Add the herbs and cook for another 2 minutes.
6. Meantime, make the cheese sauce. Melt the butter in a medium saucepan, add the flour and whisk until smooth, forming a roux.
7. Gradually add the milk, 250 ml at a time, whisking constantly to prevent lumps. Cook until the roux is smooth after every addition.
8. Continue to simmer and whisk over medium heat for about 10 minutes until the sauce is thick, smooth and creamy.
9. Stir in the cheese until melted and season with the salt and pepper.
10. To cook the conchigliette, bring the water to the boil in a large saucepan and add the remaining 5 ml salt.
11. Add the pasta to the boiling water and cook, uncovered, for 5–10 minutes until al dente.
12. Switch on the oven's grill.
13. Drain the pasta and tip it into a serving dish. Spoon over the mince and spread the cheese sauce over the top. Grill until lightly browned.
14. Serve garnished with fresh origanum.

This creamy pasta dish goes well with a simple mixed leaf salad (see page 46). It is quick to prepare and ideal for when you do not have much time to cook.

FETTUCCINI
Alfredo

SERVES 4–6

5 ml salt
500 g homemade fettuccini (see page 108)
15 ml butter
500 ml cream
500 ml grated Parmesan cheese
freshly ground black pepper to taste
fresh origanum to garnish

1. Half-fill a large saucepan with water, add the salt and bring to the boil.
2. Add the pasta to the boiling water and cook for 5 minutes until al dente.
3. While the pasta is cooking, heat the butter and cream in a separate saucepan.
4. Drain the pasta and return it to the saucepan on the stove, over low heat.
5. Add the cream mixture and half of the Parmesan cheese and stir until the cream thickens. Season with black pepper to taste.
6. Serve in pasta bowls, sprinkled with a generous helping of the remaining Parmesan and garnished with fresh origanum.

My son has an Italian friend whose grandfather always says, 'Parmesan should be spread like an avalanche over your pasta!' Always use fresh Parmesan cheese and grate it just before serving.

FETTUCCINI
Carbonara

SERVES 4

250 g bacon, diced
5 ml salt
400 g homemade fettuccini (see page 108)
3 extra-large eggs
430 ml grated Parmesan cheese
125 ml cream
freshly ground black pepper to taste
fresh origanum and basil leaves to garnish

1. Fry the bacon in a frying pan over medium heat until cooked. Drain on paper towel and set aside.
2. Half-fill a large saucepan with water, add the salt and bring to the boil.
3. Cook the fettuccini in the boiling water for 5 minutes until al dente.
4. While the pasta is cooking, whisk the eggs in a medium bowl and add 180 ml of the Parmesan cheese, followed by the cream and bacon. Mix well.
5. Drain the pasta and return to the saucepan with a little water (just to wet it) to keep warm.
6. Stir in the egg mixture and mix well until the sauce thickens. Season with pepper to taste.
7. Serve immediately with the rest of the grated Parmesan and garnished with fresh origanum and basil leaves.

PENNE
with chicken
and mushrooms

30 ml olive oil

1 onion, diced

125 g white button
   mushrooms, sliced

3 deboned skinless
   chicken breasts

salt and freshly ground black
   pepper to taste

125 ml white wine

30 ml tomato paste

250 ml cream

500 g penne

250 ml finely grated
   Parmesan cheese

fresh origanum to garnish

1. Heat half the oil in a large frying pan and sauté the onion until cooked.
2. Add mushrooms and sauté until softened. Remove the onion and mushrooms from the pan and set aside.
3. Flatten the chicken breasts with a meat mallet and cut into thin strips, 3–4 cm long.
4. Reheat the same frying pan, add the remaining oil and lightly fry the chicken until just cooked.
5. Add the onion and mushrooms to the chicken and season to taste.
6. Add the wine and tomato paste and bring to the boil.
7. Add the cream, turn down the heat and reduce until the sauce has thickened.
8. Half-fill a large saucepan with water and bring to the boil, adding 5 ml salt.
9. Cook the penne in the boiling water for 5–8 minutes until al dente.
10. Drain the pasta and return to the saucepan.
11. Add the chicken and mushroom sauce and stir through.
12. Tip into a serving dish and garnish with the grated Parmesan and fresh origanum.

POTATO GNOCCHI
with creamed mushrooms

500 g potatoes, peeled
    and diced
500 ml water
15 ml butter
1 extra-large egg, whisked
250 ml cake flour, sifted
5 ml salt

CREAMED MUSHROOMS
15 ml olive oil
1 onion, diced
250 g white button
    mushrooms, sliced
250 ml cream
salt and freshly ground black
    pepper to taste
250 ml grated Parmesan
    cheese
fresh origanum to garnish

1. Place the potatoes and water in a saucepan, cover with a lid and boil for 15–20 minutes until soft.
2. Drain and then mash the potatoes by hand or purée in a food processor.
3. Allow to cool, then tip into a mixing bowl and stir in the butter.
4. Add the whisked egg and stir in the flour, mixing to form a dough.
5. Cover the bowl with cling wrap and refrigerate for 90 minutes.
6. To make the creamed mushrooms, heat the oil in a large frying pan and sauté the onion until soft.
7. Add the mushrooms and sauté until cooked.
8. Pour in the cream and simmer until the sauce has slightly reduced and thickened. Season to taste.
9. Spoon a small handful of potato dough onto a floured surface and roll into a long sausage, 1.5 cm thick. Cut the sausage into 1.5 cm thick pillows.
10. Using a fork, lightly press down on each pillow and gently pull the fork towards you to create a classic gnocchi shape. Place the gnocchi on a floured breadboard while you cut and shape the rest of the dough.
11. In the meantime, half-fill a large saucepan with water and bring to the boil, adding the 5 ml salt.
12. Lift the breadboard over the boiling water and gently push some gnocchi into the water. Don't overcrowd; rather cook in batches.
13. Cook the gnocchi for 1–2 minutes. They are cooked when they rise to the surface of the water.
14. Lift out the gnocchi with a slotted spoon and keep them warm in a serving dish while you cook the rest.
15. Reheat the creamed mushrooms if necessary and stir through the gnocchi in the serving dish.
16. Serve garnished with the grated Parmesan and fresh origanum.

This is a heart-warming winter meal in one bowl.

SPAGHETTI
bolognaise

SERVES 4

15 ml olive oil

1 onion, chopped

4 cloves garlic, chopped

500 g beef mince

410 g can chopped peeled
   tomatoes

50 g tomato paste

1 large carrot, coarsely grated

125 ml dry red wine

5 ml brown sugar

10 ml salt and freshly ground
   black pepper to taste

15 ml dried Italian herbs

2 litres water

400 g homemade spaghetti
   (see page 108)

250 ml grated Parmesan
   cheese

fresh origanum to garnish

1. Heat the oil in a medium saucepan with a lid and sauté the onion until soft.
2. Add the garlic and sauté for 1 minute.
3. Add the mince and fry over high heat, stirring continuously, for 5–10 minutes until just cooked and loose.
4. Pulp the tomatoes with a pestle in a jug and add to the mince along with the tomato paste, carrot, wine and sugar. Season with 5 ml salt and black pepper to taste.
5. Put on the lid and simmer for 10 minutes until the meat juices have thickened.
6. Stir in the herbs and cook for another 2 minutes.
7. Bring the water to the boil in a separate saucepan and add 5 ml salt.
8. Cook the spaghetti in the boiling water for 5–10 minutes until it is al dente.
9. Drain the spaghetti in a colander and serve topped with bolognaise, grated Parmesan and fresh origanum in pasta bowls.

You can substitute 125 ml water for the wine.

SPAGHETTI
primavera

SERVES 4–6

15 ml butter

1 onion, diced

1 stalk celery, diced

250 ml frozen peas

375 ml cream

250 ml grated Parmesan cheese

freshly ground black pepper to taste

5 ml salt

500 g homemade spaghetti (see page 108)

1. Melt the butter in a medium saucepan and sauté the onion and celery until softened.
2. Add the peas, cream and half the Parmesan cheese and simmer until thickened.
3. Season to taste with black pepper.
4. Half-fill a large saucepan with water, bring to the boil and add 5 ml salt.
5. Cook the spaghetti in the boiling water for 5–10 minutes until al dente, then drain and return it to the saucepan.
6. Stir in the sauce and serve in pasta bowls, garnished with the remaining Parmesan.

TAGLIATELLE
with bacon, white wine and mushroom sauce

SERVES 4

15 ml butter

125–250 g back or shoulder bacon, cut into 2 cm squares

1 onion, finely diced

5 ml crushed garlic

250 g white button mushrooms, thinly sliced

a splash of white wine

200 ml double cream

salt and freshly ground black pepper to taste

300 g homemade tagliatelle (see page 108)

60 ml grated Parmesan cheese

fresh origanum to garnish

1. Melt the butter in a medium saucepan and fry the bacon until cooked.
2. Add the onion and garlic and sauté until softened.
3. Add the mushrooms and sauté until cooked.
4. Pour in a splash of white wine and cook until the liquid has reduced.
5. Add the cream, then season to taste and cook until the sauce has thickened.
6. Half-fill a large saucepan with water, bring to the boil and add 5 ml salt.
7. Cook the tagliatelle in the boiling water for 5 minutes until al dente, then drain and return it to the saucepan.
8. Pour the sauce over the pasta and gently mix.
9. Serve in pasta bowls garnished with the grated Parmesan cheese and fresh origanum.

COUNTRY FOOD SHOP

FUDGE

KOFFIE & KOEKSISTERS

BELGIAN TRUFFLES

VEGETABLES AND SIDES

There are many ways to cook vegetables. Some people prefer them slightly crunchy while others prefer softer, slow-cooked vegetables. I have included a variety of cooking methods to suit every style. I always serve a yellow and a green vegetable together, and definitely never two vegetables of the same colour. Although we do not have starch with every meal, I have given you a variety of starches here too so that you can try new combinations. I always find variation makes meals more interesting.

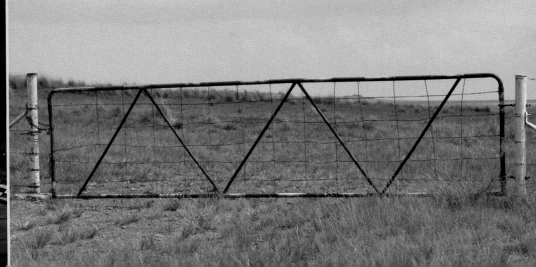

Caramelised
BABY CARROTS

15 ml butter

300 g baby carrots, unpeeled and well washed

60 ml brown sugar

2.5 ml salt

1. Heat the butter in a large frying pan with a lid over medium heat and add the carrots.
2. Season with the sugar and salt and put on the lid.
3. Turn down the heat to low and simmer until the carrots are caramelised but firm. Shake the pan to turn them.
4. Serve immediately.

BABY POTATOES
with butter and parsley

SERVES 4

500 g baby potatoes (3–4 per person)
30 ml butter
30 ml finely chopped fresh parsley
coarse sea salt to taste

1. Put the baby potatoes in a medium saucepan and cover with water. Bring to the boil and cook until soft. Drain.
2. Heat the butter in a large frying pan over medium heat and add the potatoes.
3. Fry until golden brown.
4. Add the chopped parsley and season with sea salt to taste.

Caramelised
JULIENNED CARROTS

SERVES 6–8

600 g medium–large carrots, peeled
125 ml brown sugar
30 ml butter
5 ml salt

1. Top and tail the carrots and cut them into 5 cm lengths.
2. Cut each in half lengthways, and again so you have four flat strips.
3. Cut each into 3–4 mm julienne strips.
4. Place the carrots in a large frying pan with a lid and add the sugar, butter and salt.
5. Put on the lid and heat on high for 3–5 minutes until the carrots start to cook.
6. Turn down the heat and simmer, covered, for 30 minutes until the carrots are tender.
7. Remove the lid and lightly stir to turn the carrots. If they have not yet caramelised, turn up the heat and caramelise for 3–5 minutes, ensuring they don't burn. Do not over-caramelise, as they will turn into toffee.

Julienned vegetables are vegetables that have been finely sliced into thin strips.

Caramelised CINNAMON PUMPKIN

SERVES 4–6

1 kg pumpkin, peeled and cubed

125 ml brown sugar

5 ml salt

15 ml butter

ground cinnamon to taste

1. Heat the pumpkin in a large frying pan with a lid until it starts to cook.
2. Turn down the heat to low and add the sugar and salt.
3. Put on the lid and simmer until soft.
4. Add the butter, turn the heat to medium and fry the pumpkin until lightly browned.
5. Sprinkle over cinnamon to taste and stir. If the pumpkin is dry, add 60 ml water.
6. Now caramelise over medium heat. The pumpkin will break up when you stir it.

Creamed
GREEN BEAN STEW

350 g green beans
1 large potato, peeled
1 small onion, diced
5 ml salt
500 ml water
45 ml cream
2.5 ml freshly ground black pepper

1. Top and tail the beans. Holding one small bunch of beans at a time, finely slice them to 2 mm thick.
2. Slice the potato into 4 mm thick discs.
3. Place the beans, potato, onion, salt and water in a medium saucepan with a lid.
4. Bring to the boil over high heat, then turn down the heat and simmer, covered, for 30–45 minutes until the beans are soft and the water has cooked away completely.
5. Mash the beans and potato with the cream and black pepper.

This goes really well with caramelised cinnamon pumpkin (see page 131).

Creamed
POTATO BAKE

SERVES 6–8

1.2 kg medium potatoes (about 8)

5 ml salt

freshly ground black pepper to taste

125 ml grated Parmesan or Cheddar cheese

250 ml cream

1. Place the potatoes, skin on, in a large saucepan. Cover with water and gently boil until slightly softened.
2. Preheat the oven to 180 ˚C.
3. Drain the potatoes and allow them to cool slightly before peeling (this is optional).
4. Cut the potatoes into 5–7 mm thick slices.
5. Using a 20 x 30 cm roasting dish, pack the potato slices at an angle in rows, like dominoes.
6. Season with the salt and pepper to taste and cover with the grated cheese.
7. Pour over the cream and bake for 30 minutes until the potatoes are cooked and the cream has thickened.

When we braai at the weekend and do not feel like pap as a starch, I love to make this dish as the creamy potatoes go very well with any grilled meat.

Creamed SPINACH

300 g Swiss chard or spinach leaves, stems removed

1 onion, diced

1 medium potato, peeled and sliced

5 ml salt

500 ml water

60–125 ml cream

freshly ground black pepper to taste

1. Cut the chard or spinach leaves into 1 cm strips.
2. Place the onion, potato and salt in a medium saucepan. Add the water and bring to the boil.
3. Simmer over medium heat for 20–30 minutes until the potato is soft.
4. Add the spinach and cook until wilted.
5. Drain completely and mash with enough cream to form a consistency like soft mashed potatoes. It should not be too runny. Season to taste with black pepper.
6. Simmer over low heat for 5 minutes before serving.

Children don't always like spinach, but mine love this creamed version.

Creamy
MASHED POTATOES

8 medium potatoes, peeled and sliced

5 ml salt

125 ml milk

125 ml grated Parmesan cheese

15 ml butter

1. Cook the potatoes in a medium saucepan of water until soft.
2. Drain, add the salt and mash with a potato masher. Strain the mash through a sieve if it is not smooth enough.
3. Heat the milk separately and then add to the mash along with the cheese and butter.
4. Beat the mash with a wooden spoon for 1 minute until creamy. If the mash is still a bit starchy, add a little more milk. It should, however, hold its shape when scooped onto a plate.

This mashed potato is extremely creamy and complements any dish. It can be served with creamy haddock or meats like lamb shank or stew, but to my family it is best served with boerewors. They are delighted when they hear we're having mash and wors, my South African take on English bangers and mash.

Honey-basted OVEN-ROASTED VEGETABLES

SERVES 4–6

1 sweet red pepper, deseeded and flattened

1 sweet yellow pepper, deseeded and flattened

500 g butternut

1 large onion, quartered

30 ml olive oil

15 ml honey

5 ml coarse sea salt

1. Preheat the oven to 260 ˚C and switch on the top grill.
2. Place the flattened peppers, skin side up, on a greased baking tray and grill until partially blackened. Cover with cling wrap and allow to cool slightly, then remove and discard the skins.
3. Cut the peppers into 3 x 4 cm squares and set aside.
4. Turn down the oven to 180 ˚C and turn off the grill.
5. Slice the butternut into 1.5 cm thick discs, peel off the skin and slice each disc in half.
6. Place the butternut on a clean baking tray and add the onion, loosening the leaves.
7. Drizzle over the olive oil and bake for 30 minutes until the butternut is soft. Turn halfway through cooking and add the peppers.
8. Drizzle over the honey and bake for another 10 minutes. Season with the salt before serving.

This is a modern, delicious and quick alternative to slow-cooked vegetables.

Oven-baked
POTATO WEDGES

1 medium potato per person
olive oil to drizzle
rosemary and olive salt to taste

1. Preheat the oven to 225 ˚C.
2. Cut each potato in half lengthways and then into 2 cm thick wedges.
3. Place in a microwavable dish and cover with cling wrap.
4. Microwave on high for 10 minutes.
5. Remove the cling wrap and turn out onto a greased baking tray. Lightly drizzle with olive oil and season with rosemary and olive salt.
6. Bake in the oven for 15–20 minutes, turning once or twice, until crispy on the outside.
7. Serve immediately.

These wedges can replace fried chips as a healthier option. You can also serve them as tapas in a bowl with a dip on the side. Add two extra potatoes for every four additional people.

Duck fat
ROAST POTATOES

**6–8 medium potatoes, peeled
and quartered**
100 ml cake flour
330 g duck fat
salt to taste

1. Cook the potatoes in a saucepan of water, covered, until soft. Drain well.
2. Sprinkle the flour over the potatoes and shake around to coat.
3. Preheat the oven to 200 °C.
4. Heat the duck fat in a roasting dish in the oven for 5 minutes.
5. Add the potatoes and bake for 15 minutes.
6. Turn the potatoes and swirl them around in the fat before baking for another 15 minutes.
7. Turn again and bake for a further 10 minutes until golden and crispy.
8. Drain the potatoes on paper towel and season with salt.
9. Serve immediately.

These go well with roasts like leg of lamb or gammon.

BUTTERNUT FRITTERS
with caramel sauce

SERVES 10–12

about 1 kg butternut, peeled
   and cubed
5 ml salt
2 extra-large eggs
250 ml cake flour, sifted
10 ml baking powder
750 ml sunflower oil

CARAMEL SAUCE
125 g butter
250 ml white sugar
250 ml water
250 ml milk
5 ml vanilla essence
45 ml cornflour
a pinch of salt

1. Place the butternut and salt in a large saucepan with a tight-fitting lid. Cover and heat until it starts to cook, then turn down the heat and let it steam for about 30 minutes until soft. Drain if necessary.
2. Mash the butternut and leave to cool completely. You should have about 750 ml.
3. Place the butternut and eggs in a large mixing bowl and mix well.
4. Add the flour and baking powder and combine.
5. Line a large rectangular dish with paper towel and place it next to the stovetop.
6. Heat the oil in a large frying pan over medium heat.
7. Place golf-ball-size dollops of the butternut mixture into the hot oil and fry for 3–4 minutes on each side until slightly browned.
8. Gently lift the fritters out of the oil using two forks and place them on the paper towel to drain.
9. Continue until you have used up all the mixture.
10. To make the caramel sauce, melt the butter and sugar in a medium saucepan over medium heat. Stir until the sugar has dissolved and then leave to caramelise. Keep an eye on it, as you don't want the sugar to burn. You only want it to be a caramel colour.
11. Mix the remaining ingredients in a bowl and add to the caramel.
12. Stir until all the lumps have dissolved and cook for 4–5 minutes until translucent.
13. Place the fritters in rows in a large heated serving dish, pour over the caramel sauce and serve immediately.

You can serve these butternut fritters with either the caramel sauce or cinnamon sugar. When serving with cinnamon sugar, sprinkle over the sugar as soon as you've placed the fritters on the paper towel.

RATATOUILLE

1 small aubergine, sliced
olive oil to grill
1 red onion, cut into eighths
1 red sweet pepper, deseeded and cubed
1 yellow sweet pepper, deseeded and cubed
4 medium baby marrows, sliced
3 cloves garlic
2 x 410 g cans peeled Italian tomatoes, chopped
15 ml balsamic vinegar
10 ml brown sugar
5 ml salt
freshly ground black pepper to taste

1. Heat a griddle pan over high heat.
2. Brush the aubergine slices with olive oil and lightly grill on both sides. Remove from the heat and cut into quarters. Set aside.
3. Heat 15 ml olive oil in a large frying pan and sauté the onion, peppers, baby marrows and garlic until softened.
4. Add the aubergine, tomatoes, balsamic vinegar, sugar, salt and black pepper.
5. Simmer for 10 minutes, uncovered, to reduce the liquid.
6. Serve warm.

I love to serve this dish with grilled chicken and basmati rice.

SWEET POTATOES
in butter and ginger syrup

SERVES 4–6

500 g sweet potatoes, peeled

100 g butter

60 ml brown sugar

60 ml golden syrup

2.5 ml salt

2.5 ml grated dried or ground ginger

1. Cut the sweet potatoes into 5 mm-thick slices.
2. Heat a large frying pan with a lid over high heat.
3. Add the sweet potatoes and the remaining ingredients, turn down the heat, put on the lid and simmer until the syrup is reduced, thick and glossy.
4. Stir through once and serve hot.

Baked whole
SWEET POTATOES

1 medium sweet potato per person
5 ml butter per person
salt to taste

1. Preheat the oven to 180 ˚C.
2. Wash the sweet potatoes and prick each one a few times with a knife.
3. Place them on the middle rack of the oven and bake for about 1 hour until soft inside.
4. Remove from the oven, cut open and dress with butter and salt.

These are delicious served with snoek.

Basmati RICE

250 ml basmati rice
500 ml water
5 ml salt

1. Bring the basmati rice, water and salt to the boil in a medium saucepan with a tight-fitting lid. Do not stir.
2. Turn down the heat to low–medium and put on the lid.
3. Steam for 10–15 minutes until the water has completely evaporated and the rice is cooked.

Try basmati with its oriental flavour instead of plain rice when you next have a curry. It also goes well with chicken dishes.

MEALIE PAP
tart

1.625 litres water

7.5 ml salt

625 ml good-quality
   mealie meal

100 g butter

410 g can whole kernel
   corn, drained

15 ml olive oil

250 g bacon, diced

15 ml butter

500 g button mushrooms,
   sliced

500–750 ml grated Cheddar
   cheese

SAUCE

15 ml olive oil

1 onion, diced

4 tomatoes, diced

5 ml brown sugar

30 ml cake flour

60 ml chutney

30 ml Worcestershire sauce

30 ml tomato sauce

375 ml water

salt and freshly ground black
   pepper to taste

1. Bring the water and salt to the boil in a large saucepan with a lid.
2. Add the mealie meal and briskly stir with a whisk until all the lumps have dissolved. (Do not add the mealie meal if the water is bubbling too vigorously. If it is, remove the pan from the heat until it stops, turn down the heat, return the pan to the stove and then add the mealie meal.)
3. Put on the lid and turn down the heat to low. Let it cook for 30–45 minutes, stirring once or twice with a wooden spoon.
4. Stir the 100 g butter and corn into the pap. Keep on a low heat until needed.
5. Preheat the oven to 200 ˚C.
6. Heat a large frying pan, add the oil and fry the bacon until crispy. Drain on paper towel and set aside.
7. Add the 15 ml butter to the same frying pan and fry the mushrooms until golden. Set aside.
8. To make the sauce, heat the olive oil in a separate large frying pan and sauté the onion.
9. Add the tomatoes and fry until soft.
10. Stir in the sugar and flour, and then add the chutney, Worcestershire sauce and tomato sauce. Season with salt and black pepper.
11. Add the water, stir well and simmer until the sauce is reduced and thick.
12. Grease a 20 x 30 cm rectangular ovenproof dish and spread half of the pap over the base.
13. Evenly spread over half of the sauce, and then scatter over half the mushrooms, bacon and cheese. Repeat the layers.
14. Bake for 15–20 minutes until the cheese has melted and browned.

Serve with braaied meat and salad.

MELKKOS

1 litre full-cream milk

80 g butter

125 ml cake flour

2.5 ml salt

250 ml white sugar mixed with 30 ml ground cinnamon

1. Bring the milk to the boil in a medium saucepan.
2. Mix the butter, flour and salt until it resembles coarse flakes.
3. As soon as the milk starts to boil, add the flour mixture and stir with a whisk.
4. When it starts to thicken, turn down the heat to low and simmer for 5 minutes, stirring every minute, until cooked and glossy.
5. Serve hot in individual bowls and covered with cinnamon sugar.

Melkkos, literally 'milk food', is a wonderful winter meal when you don't feel like cooking and just want something light to warm you up. My grandmother used to make this on cold winter evenings when we'd had a big lunch during the day. The thick layer of cinnamon sugar melting from the heat of the porridge adds to the comforting flavours of this dish.

SAMP

500 ml samp
1.5 litres water
5 ml salt

1. Place the samp in a large bowl, cover with hot water and leave to stand for 30 minutes. Rinse and drain.
2. Now place the samp in a large saucepan with a tight-fitting lid, cover with water and bring to the boil, then rinse well and drain.
3. Add the 1.5 litres of water and the salt to the samp in the saucepan and cook, covered, over low heat for 3–4 hours until soft and fluffy. Do not stir, as this will make the samp mushy. It should be loose and not sticky. If it becomes dry and is not fully cooked, add another 250 ml hot water and steam until cooked.

Serve with oxtail stew, beef casserole or lamb shanks as an alternative to rice. I have found that samp cooks best in a slow-cooker. If using a slow-cooker, follow the recipe above but turn the slow-cooker to high and cook for 3–4 hours.

PEARLED WHEAT

250 ml pearled wheat
875 ml water
5 ml salt

1. Place the pearled wheat and 250 ml of the water in a medium saucepan with a lid.
2. Bring to the boil, then drain and rinse the wheat.
3. Drain once more before adding the remaining water and the salt.
4. Turn down the heat to low and simmer with the lid on for 30–40 minutes until the wheat is cooked and has doubled in volume. It takes longer to cook than rice, but should be as loose as rice.

Serve with mutton or beef roasts, smothered in brown gravy.

Saffron RICE

250 ml basmati rice
500 ml water
5 ml chicken stock powder
a pinch of saffron threads
2.5 ml salt
15 ml butter

1. Place everything except the butter in a medium saucepan with a lid and bring to the boil over high heat.
2. Turn down the heat and simmer with the lid on for 10–15 minutes until cooked.
3. Mix in the butter and serve.

Serve with steak or grilled chicken.

Spicy stir-fried RICE

250 ml long-grain rice

750 ml water

2.5 ml salt

30 ml olive oil

5–7 medium spring onions,
    finely chopped

1 medium green pepper,
    deseeded and
    finely chopped

1 medium red pepper,
    deseeded and
    finely chopped

125 g button mushrooms,
    finely chopped

60 ml finely chopped
    fresh parsley

30 ml rice spice

30 ml butter

1. Bring the rice and 250 ml of the water to the boil in a medium saucepan with a tight-fitting lid. Drain, rinse and discard all the liquid.

2. Add the remaining water and the salt, put on the lid and simmer over low heat for 20–30 minutes until the rice is cooked and swollen.

3. Heat the oil in a large frying pan with a lid and sauté the onions for 2 minutes.

4. Add the peppers and sauté for a further 2–4 minutes.

5. Add the mushrooms and sauté for another 2–4 minutes.

6. Add the parsley and then stir the rice spice into the vegetables.

7. Drain the rice and add to the vegetables. Mix well.

8. Stir in the butter until melted and then turn off the heat. Cover with the lid and let it rest and steam for another 5–10 minutes.

This doesn't need gravy, as it is moist and buttery. Serve with steak, roast, fish or grilled poultry.

Sundried tomato and feta
COUSCOUS

SERVES 6–8

15 ml olive oil

1 onion, diced

750 ml couscous

15 ml chicken stock powder

2.5 ml salt

enough water to cover

80 g sundried tomatoes in vinaigrette

115 g plain feta cheese, crumbled

10 ml paprika

30 ml butter

1. Heat the olive oil in a medium saucepan and sauté the onion. Set aside.
2. Place the couscous in a separate saucepan with a tight-fitting lid, add the stock powder, salt and enough water to cover the couscous.
3. Put on the lid and let it steam over low heat until all the liquid has evaporated. This only takes 3–4 minutes.
4. Drain the sundried tomatoes and cut them into 1 cm pieces.
5. Stir the onion, sundried tomatoes, feta and paprika into the couscous.
6. Add the butter and stir through until melted.
7. Serve immediately.

Serve with grilled chicken, red meat or roasts. For a variation, add Spanish smoked paprika to give it a smoky taste.

Turmeric
RICE

SERVES 4–6

250 ml white rice
750 ml water
5 ml turmeric
5 ml salt
50 ml raisins (optional)

1. Bring the rice and 250 ml of the water to the boil in a medium saucepan with a tight-fitting lid. Drain, rinse and discard all the liquid.
2. Add the remaining water, turmeric, salt and raisins (if using) to the rice and bring to the boil.
3. Turn down the heat to low, put on the lid and simmer for 20 minutes until the rice is cooked and fluffy.

This is great served with bobotie (see page 191).

FISH AND SEAFOOD

Our family used to fish during summer holidays on the South Coast. There are only a few things that can match the taste of fish, fresh from the sea, cleaned, cooked and enjoyed the same day. My children have fond memories of when their grandfathers and dad used to come home from a day on the open ocean with the catch of the day. Since we prefer holidaying in the Cape these days, we buy fish from a market or fishery, but only one that guarantees fresh fish caught that day. Our favourites are hake, barracuda and dorado. When buying fresh fish, the eyes of the fish should be clear and not milky and the flesh should be firm, not flaky.

Tapas-style
FISH FINGERS

SERVES 4–6

500 g fresh hake fillets, skinless and deboned

250 ml cake flour

30 ml fish spice

2 extra-large eggs

60 ml water

500 ml canola oil

salad cream to serve

1. Cut the fish into finger-size portions.
2. Mix the flour and fish spice in a medium bowl.
3. Beat the eggs and water in a separate medium bowl.
4. Place all the fish in the egg mixture and leave until the oil is ready.
5. Heat the oil in a large frying pan over medium–high heat.
6. One by one, take the fish fingers from the egg mixture, dip them into the flour mixture and then back into the egg mixture.
7. Fry the fish fingers for 3–4 minutes and then drain them on 2–3 layers of paper towel.
8. Serve with salad cream on the side for dipping.

When my son catches fish and it's not enough for a main meal, I fillet it and serve it tapas-style as a starter. You could of course serve these as a main with vegetable croquettes and crudités. Any fresh-caught fish will do.

Fried
FRESH HAKE

SERVES 4–6

250 ml cake flour

30 ml fish spice

2 extra-large eggs

60 ml cream

500 g fresh hake fillets

500–750 ml canola oil

lemon wedges and tartar sauce (see page 305) to serve

1. Mix the flour and fish spice in a bowl large enough to roll the fish.
2. Beat the eggs and cream in a separate bowl also large enough to accommodate the fish.
3. Place all the fish fillets in the egg mixture and leave until the oil is ready.
4. Heat the oil in a large frying pan over medium heat.
5. One by one, take the fillets from the egg mixture and dip them into the flour mixture, covering both sides well.
6. Fry in the oil for 3–4 minutes on each side and then drain on 2–3 layers of paper towel.
7. Serve immediately with lemon wedges and tartar sauce.

Hake is the most commonly bought fish and also one of the tastiest when fresh. You can use any fresh fish for this recipe.

Salmon
FISH CAKES

MAKES 8–10

2 x 213 g cans whole salmon

½ small onion, finely chopped

45 ml chopped fresh parsley

2 extra-large eggs

10 ml baking powder

15 ml bottled capers

375 ml toasted breadcrumbs

250 ml sunflower oil

creamy mayonnaise and
lemon wedges to serve

1. Remove all the bones from the salmon and flake the fish with a fork.
2. Place the salmon, onion, parsley, eggs, baking powder, capers and 125 ml of the breadcrumbs in a medium mixing bowl and mix well.
3. Form the mixture into fish cakes with the help of a small scone cutter.
4. Spread the remaining breadcrumbs on a large plate and roll each fish cake in the crumbs to coat all sides.
5. Transfer the fish cakes to a floured dish. Refrigerate for 10 minutes.
6. Heat the oil in a large frying pan over medium–high heat.
7. Fry the fish cakes on each side until golden brown and drain on paper towel.
8. Serve with creamy mayonnaise, lemon wedges and a side salad.

Seafood
PAELLA

SERVES 4–6

450 g mussels in shells,
   cleaned
300 g prawn tails, cleaned
300 g calamari rings
200 g hake fillet
30 ml olive oil
1 onion, diced
1 small red pepper,
   deseeded and diced
1 small green pepper,
   deseeded and diced
3 cloves garlic, chopped
5 ml Spanish smoked paprika
250 ml Arborio rice
5 ml saffron threads
5 ml salt
500–625 ml chicken stock
100 g butter
juice of 1 lemon
125 ml frozen peas
chopped fresh flat-leaf
   parsley to garnish
lemon wedges to serve

1. If the seafood is frozen, thaw it first. Drain any water from the seafood before using. Cut the hake into 2 x 2 cm squares.
2. Heat the oil in an extra-large frying pan or paella pan with a tight-fitting lid and sauté the onion and peppers until soft.
3. Add the garlic and sauté for another minute, then add the paprika and cook for 30 seconds.
4. Add the rice, saffron, salt and 250 ml chicken stock and cook over high heat, uncovered, for 5–7 minutes until the liquid has reduced. Do not stir the rice while cooking.
5. Add another 125 ml stock and allow to cook for 5 minutes or until absorbed.
6. Repeat until either all the stock has been used or the rice is soft and not grainy.
7. In a separate large frying pan, heat the butter and drizzle in the lemon juice.
8. Quickly sauté the mussels over high heat until their shells open. Set aside in a bowl, discarding the mussels that haven't opened.
9. In the same pan, fry the prawns over high heat until they turn pink. Set aside in a bowl.
10. In the same pan, quickly sauté the calamari until just cooked. The longer you cook the calamari, the tougher it will become.
11. Add the peas and hake to the rice and steam with the lid on for 2 minutes until the fish turns white. Stir through once.
12. Add the mussels, prawns and calamari to the rice and stir through.
13. Garnish with parsley and serve immediately with lemon wedges.

Arborio rice works best in this recipe as real Spanish rice is hard to find. The Arborio gives the dish a lot of moisture. You can use either fresh or frozen seafood.

BRAAIED SNOEK
with sweet barbecue marinade

SERVES 4–6

1 large whole snoek, filleted
    and halved lengthways
125 ml meat marinade
60 ml chutney
60 ml apricot jam

1. Prepare a slow-burning braai fire. The snoek should be cooked over medium heat.
2. Line a folding grid with heavy-duty foil and place the snoek halves, flesh-side up, parallel on the grid.
3. Mix the meat marinade, chutney and apricot jam in a small bowl.
4. Baste the flesh of the snoek with this marinade, close the foil over the fish and close the grid. Fasten the handles of the grid so that it can be turned.
5. Grill the snoek for about 5 minutes on each side until just cooked.
6. Serve with baked whole sweet potatoes (see page 144) and salad.

Fish cooks quickly, so do not overcook the snoek as it will become dry. If there are any leftovers, keep them in the fridge to snack on the next day.

Friendship: Friends are the people we choose to do life with!

CHICKEN

Chicken is really versatile and can be cooked in so many ways. Grilled, fried, curried … every method delivers a completely different outcome. As chicken is less pricey than red meat and, some would argue, the healthier option, it is worth cooking every which way.

CHICKEN MAYONNAISE
and sautéed mushrooms on health bread

15 ml olive oil

2 skinless deboned chicken
   breasts

salt and freshly ground black
   pepper to taste

125 ml salad cream or
   mayonnaise (I prefer
   salad cream, as it is not
   overly tangy)

5 ml sugar

2.5 ml hot English mustard
   powder

15 ml butter, plus extra
   to serve

250 g white button
   mushrooms, sliced

4 slices health bread
   (see page 84)

salad leaves to serve

1. Heat the oil in a medium frying pan over high heat.
2. Slightly flatten the chicken breasts with a meat mallet on a wooden board.
3. Fry the chicken breasts on both sides until cooked, season and transfer to a plate to cool, before slicing and flaking.
4. Mix the chicken with the salad cream or mayonnaise, sugar and mustard powder in a bowl.
5. In a clean frying pan, melt the butter and sauté the mushrooms until softened.
6. Toast and butter the health bread and arrange a layer of salad leaves on each slice.
7. Spoon chicken mayonnaise onto each slice and top with warm sautéed mushrooms.
8. Season and serve immediately.

Butter CHICKEN

SERVES 4

4 large skinned deboned
  chicken breasts, cut into
  2 cm cubes
juice of 1 lemon
15 ml cake flour
30 ml olive oil
1 onion, finely chopped
5 ml crushed garlic
5 ml chopped fresh ginger
15 ml turmeric
2.5 ml masala
5 ml salt
125 ml chicken stock
15 ml ground almonds
30 ml tomato paste
125 ml plain yoghurt
125 ml cream
fresh coriander to garnish

1. Place the chicken in a large mixing bowl, drizzle over the lemon juice and cover with the flour. Mix well.
2. Heat a large frying pan over medium heat and add the olive oil.
3. Sauté the onion until soft and stir in the garlic and ginger.
4. Stir in the turmeric and masala and fry for 30 seconds.
5. Add the chicken and fry for 3–5 minutes until just cooked.
6. Add the salt, turn down the heat to low and add the chicken stock and almonds.
7. Stir in the tomato paste and cook for 1 minute.
8. Add the yoghurt and cream and cook until the sauce has thickened and reduced.
9. Garnish with fresh coriander and serve with steamed basmati rice and chutney.

This is not a chicken curry – here the curry takes a backseat and the turmeric is the star. This dish is named butter chicken not because it contains a lot of butter, but because the chicken is so tender that it melts like soft butter in your mouth. Serve with steamed basmati rice (see page 145).

CHICKEN
à la king

SERVES 4

1.3 kg whole chicken

10 ml chicken stock powder

1 litre water

15 ml olive oil

1 onion, diced

1 small green pepper,
   deseeded and diced

250 g button mushrooms,
   sliced

15 ml cake flour

5 ml salt

freshly ground black
   pepper to taste

1 egg yolk

125 ml cream

chopped fresh parsley
   to garnish

LONG-GRAIN WHITE RICE

250 ml long-grain white rice

750 ml water

5 ml salt

1. Place the whole chicken, stock powder and water in a large saucepan with a lid and bring to the boil. Turn the heat to medium and simmer, covered, for 45–60 minutes until the chicken is cooked.
2. Remove the chicken and reserve the stock for later.
3. Debone and skin the chicken, keeping the meat only.
4. Start cooking the rice. Place the rice and 250 ml of the water in a medium saucepan with a tight-fitting lid. Bring to the boil, then rinse and drain.
5. Add the remaining water and the salt to the rice and bring to the boil once more.
6. Turn down the heat to low, put on the lid and simmer for 20 minutes until cooked and fluffy.
7. Heat the olive oil in a separate large saucepan with a lid and sauté the onion and green pepper until soft.
8. Add the mushrooms and fry until cooked.
9. Add the chicken and flour to the pan and stir.
10. Add 750 ml of the reserved chicken stock and stir.
11. Put on the lid and cook over medium heat for 5 minutes until the sauce is reduced and thick.
12. Season with the salt and pepper to taste, turn down the heat to low and stir in the egg yolk. Remove from heat to prevent the egg yolk from curdling.
13. Just before serving, reheat and stir in the cream.
14. Garnish with parsley and serve on the long-grain white rice.

CHICKEN curry

SERVES 4

30 ml olive oil

1 large onion, diced

2 cloves garlic, chopped

2.5 ml cumin seeds

5–6 cardamom pods

5 ml medium curry powder

5 ml turmeric

5 ml ground cinnamon

4 large skinned deboned
   chicken breasts, cubed

5 ml salt

5 ml brown sugar

5 ml chicken stock powder

250 ml water

40 ml desiccated coconut,
   plus extra to serve

125 ml cream or coconut
   milk (optional)

1. Heat half the olive oil in a medium saucepan with a lid over medium heat and sauté the onion.
2. Add the garlic and sauté for another minute.
3. Grind the cumin and cardamom in a mortar and pestle and discard the cardamom shells.
4. Add the remaining oil to the onion, along with the curry powder, turmeric, cinnamon and ground spices. Fry for 30 seconds.
5. Add the chicken and fry for 5–8 minutes until cooked.
6. Add the salt and sugar.
7. Mix the chicken stock powder into the water and add to the pan.
8. Add the coconut, mix well, put on the lid and simmer for 20 minutes.
9. Stir in the cream or coconut milk, if using, and reduce for 5 minutes before serving with extra desiccated coconut, rice and chutney.

This is a mild curry. For a stronger curry, adjust the amount of curry powder. Adding the cream or coconut milk near the end will make a milder, creamier curry.

Chicken STIR-FRY

SERVES 6

500 g skinned deboned
   chicken breasts
125 ml cake flour
10 ml salt
45 ml canola oil
1 onion, sliced
4 cloves garlic, roughly
   chopped
5 ml chopped or grated
   fresh ginger
1 small green pepper,
   deseeded and julienned
1 small red pepper, deseeded
   and julienned
200 g carrots, peeled
   and julienned
200 g small baby marrows,
   julienned
100 g button mushrooms,
   sliced
freshly ground black
   pepper to taste
30 ml cake flour
10 ml chicken stock powder
625 ml water
15 ml dark soy sauce
15 ml honey
1.25 ml sesame oil

1. Beat the chicken breasts to a thickness of 1 cm and cut into strips.
2. Mix the 125 ml flour with half the salt in a large bowl. Add the chicken and toss to coat.
3. Heat half of the oil in large saucepan or wok.
4. Add the chicken and stir-fry for 2–3 minutes until just cooked.
5. Remove the chicken with a slotted spoon and set aside in a separate bowl.
6. In the same pan, heat the remaining oil and sauté the onion, garlic and ginger.
7. Stirring continuously, add the peppers and sauté for 2 minutes.
8. Add the carrots and baby marrows and sauté for 2 minutes.
9. Add the mushrooms and sauté for 1 minute.
10. Add the remaining salt and black pepper to taste.
11. Stir in the 30 ml flour and chicken stock powder, followed by the water, soy sauce, honey and sesame oil.
12. Add the chicken and simmer for 3–4 minutes until the sauce has thickened.
13. Serve hot with basmati rice, chutney and desiccated coconut.

The ginger gives this dish a slight oriental flavour. This is a delicious, quick and easy, all-in-one meal.

Crispy
CHICKEN WINGS

12 chicken wings (3 per person)
chicken spice to taste

1. Preheat the oven to 180 °C.
2. Place the chicken wings, top side down, on a drip tray in a roasting pan.
3. Season with chicken spice and bake, uncovered, for 30 minutes.
4. Turn the wings top side up and season with more chicken spice.
5. Bake for another 30 minutes or until crispy.
6. Serve immediately.

These can be served as a main meal with vegetables or on their own as a starter.

Salt-roasted CHICKEN

SERVES 4–6

1.5 kg whole chicken
olive oil
coarse sea salt

1. Preheat the oven to 180 °C.
2. Rub the whole chicken with olive oil and salt.
3. Place the chicken, breast-side down, on a drip tray in a roasting pan.
4. Roast uncovered for 60–90 minutes until cooked, turning after 30 minutes.
5. To test if the chicken is cooked, insert a sharp knife into the breast meat. The juices should run clear.
6. Remove the chicken from the oven and let it rest uncovered for 5 minutes.
7. Cut into portions and serve with a salad and crusty bread.

I have found that chickens smaller than 1.3 kg cook in an hour, while those larger than 1.3 kg take 90 minutes.

Parmesan-crumbed
CHICKEN BREASTS

SERVES 4

4 skinned deboned chicken
   breasts

salt to taste

125 ml cake flour

2 extra-large eggs

125 ml finely grated
   Parmesan cheese

125 ml toasted breadcrumbs

60 ml cooking oil

salad cream for serving

1. Beat the chicken breasts to a thickness of 1 cm and season with salt.
2. Place the flour on a plate.
3. Beat the eggs in a medium bowl.
4. In a separate bowl, mix the cheese and breadcrumbs.
5. Heat the oil in a large frying pan over medium heat.
6. Coat each chicken breast first in flour, then dip it into the egg and finally coat in the cheese-breadcrumb mixture.
7. Fry the chicken breasts for 3–4 minutes on each side until just cooked.
8. Rest on paper towel for 5 minutes before serving warm with salad cream and vegetables.

The Parmesan cheese and breadcrumbs form a crunchy crust around the tender chicken breasts.

Lemon and thyme
ROAST CHICKEN

SERVES 4–6

a bunch of fresh thyme

50 g butter, softened

juice of ½ lemon

1.5 kg whole chicken

2 lemons, halved

5–7.5 ml salt

extra fresh thyme and lemon
wedges to serve

1. Preheat the oven to 180 °C.
2. Divide the bunch of thyme, picking the leaves from the stalks of one half and keeping the other half intact.
3. Mix the butter, picked thyme leaves and lemon juice in a small bowl.
4. With your hands, loosen the skin from the chicken breast up into the legs and push the butter mixture under the skin, spreading it to the back, over the breast and legs. Keep aside a small amount to rub over the outside of the chicken.
5. Place the intact bunch of thyme and the lemon halves into the cavity of the chicken.
6. Rub the outside with the remaining butter mixture and season the whole chicken with salt.
7. Place the chicken, breast-side down, on a drip tray in a roasting pan.
8. Roast, uncovered, for 60–90 minutes until cooked, turning halfway through cooking.
9. To test if the chicken is cooked, insert a sharp knife into the breast meat. The juices should run clear.
10. Remove the chicken from the oven and let it rest, uncovered, for 5 minutes.
11. Serve garnished with fresh thyme and lemon wedges.

Of all chicken roasts, this one is the best. Tender and succulent, infused with lemon and thyme, it makes the perfect Sunday roast. I have found that chickens smaller than 1.3 kg cook in an hour, while those larger than 1.3 kg take 90 minutes.

White wine-infused
CHICKEN PIE

SERVES 6–8

1.8 kg chicken thighs

10 ml dried mixed herbs

250 ml dry white wine

3 bay leaves

10 ml salt

40 ml cake flour

2.5 ml freshly ground
    black pepper

30 ml olive oil

250 g bacon, diced

1 onion, diced

5 ml crushed garlic

400 g roll readymade
    puff pastry

1 egg

1. Preheat the oven to 180 ˚C.
2. Place the chicken thighs, herbs, wine and bay leaves in a large roasting dish with a lid.
3. Season with 5 ml salt, cover and bake for 1 hour until cooked.
4. Switch off the oven, remove the chicken thighs and allow to cool uncovered. Reserve the stock.
5. Once cooled, pick off the chicken flesh and discard bones and skin.
6. Place the stock in a measuring jug and add water to make 1 litre.
7. Heat half the stock in a saucepan.
8. Mix half the flour with 60 ml water and add to the stock in the pan. Bring to the boil, season with the remaining salt and the black pepper, reduce the heat and simmer for 5 minutes.
9. Strain through a sieve and keep warm in a gravy boat.
10. Heat the olive oil in a large frying pan over high heat and fry the bacon.
11. Turn down the heat, add the onion and sauté until softened.
12. Add the garlic and sauté for 1 minute.
13. Add the remaining flour, chicken meat and stock. Bring to the boil, reduce the heat and simmer for 2 minutes until the sauce thickens.
14. Bring the oven back up to 180 ˚C, preferably on the thermo-fan setting. (While a thermo-fan is preferable, a conventional oven will also work.)
15. Grease a 25–35 cm round pie dish and spread the chicken mixture over the base.
16. Roll out the pastry on a floured surface to 2 cm larger than the dish.
17. Roll the pastry over the rolling pin and unroll it over the chicken and press into the sides. Trim any excess pastry with a sharp knife and make a few small incisions to allow steam to escape.
18. Beat the egg with 15 ml water and brush the top of the pastry.
19. Bake in the oven for 30–45 minutes until golden on top and serve hot with the gravy.

I prefer this chicken pie. My family calls it 'drunken chicken pie'.

Family: Family are the people we laugh with, cry with, and can be ourselves with and remain loved.

RED MEAT

Red meat is the champion of meats in South Africa and therefore I have included different cooking methods and a variety of dishes for you to try. From char-grilled on an open fire to braised and stewed, red meat forms an integral part of our food culture. Well-cured meat gives the tenderest cuts, so make sure you buy your red meat from a butcher you trust.

COTTAGE PIE

1.2 kg potatoes, peeled
and sliced
10 ml salt
125 ml grated Cheddar cheese
125 ml cream or milk
15 ml olive oil
1 onion, chopped
3 x 10 cm stalks celery,
chopped
2 cloves garlic, chopped
500 g beef mince
50 ml tomato sauce
50 ml Worcestershire sauce
50 ml chutney
freshly ground black pepper
to taste
125 ml water
250 ml frozen young peas
15 ml butter
15 ml brown sugar
125 ml grated Parmesan
cheese

1. Place the potatoes in a large saucepan with a lid and cover with water. Bring to the boil and cook, covered, for about 20 minutes, until soft. Drain, season with half the salt and mash well. Press the mashed potatoes through a sieve. Add the Cheddar cheese and cream or milk and beat with a wooden spoon until light and fluffy. Set aside.

2. Heat the olive oil over high heat in a large frying pan with a lid and sauté the onion and celery until tender. Add the garlic and sauté for another minute.

3. Add the mince and fry for 5–10 minutes, stirring continuously, until cooked and loose in texture, then turn down the heat and add the tomato sauce, Worcestershire sauce and chutney. Season with the remaining salt and pepper to taste, and mix well.

4. Add the water, put on the lid and cook for 10 minutes.

5. Place the frozen peas in a small saucepan over high heat, add the butter and sugar (no water) and cook for 3–4 minutes until just tender. Drain and add to the mince. Mix well.

6. Preheat the oven's grill.

7. Spoon the mince mixture into a 20 x 30 cm ovenproof dish and cover with the mashed potatoes.

8. Sprinkle over the Parmesan cheese and grill for 5 minutes. Serve immediately.

BOBOTIE

1 thick slice white bread

250 ml milk

30 ml olive oil

1 onion, chopped

5 ml crushed garlic

15–20 ml Robertsons Rajah®
    Mild & Spicy Curry Powder

15 ml turmeric

1 kg beef mince

10 ml salt

5 ml freshly ground
    black pepper

30 ml lemon juice

15 ml vinegar

30 ml apricot jam

90 ml chutney

100 ml seedless raisins

3 extra-large eggs

3–4 bay leaves

30 ml cake flour

5 ml beef stock powder

500 ml water

15 ml Worcestershire sauce

1. Preheat the oven to 180 °C.
2. Put the bread in a bowl with the milk to soak.
3. Heat half the olive oil in large saucepan over medium heat and sauté the onion and garlic.
4. Add the remaining olive oil, the curry powder and 12.5 ml of the turmeric to the onion and sauté for another 30 seconds.
5. Add the mince and fry over high heat for 5–10 minutes, stirring continuously, until cooked and loose in texture.
6. Turn down the heat and stir in the salt, pepper, lemon juice, vinegar, jam, chutney and raisins.
7. Drain the bread (keep the milk) and tear it into the mince. Mix well.
8. Beat 1 egg, quickly stir this into the mince mixture and remove the pan from the heat.
9. Spoon the mince into a 20 x 30 cm ovenproof dish, reserving 30 ml in the pan, and even out the top.
10. Beat the remaining eggs with the reserved milk and the remaining turmeric in a small bowl and pour over the mince in the dish.
11. Press the bay leaves halfway into the top and bake for 30 minutes until set.
12. While the bobotie is cooking, add the flour and stock powder to the reserved mince mixture in the pan. Bring to a high heat while adding the water and stir until thickened. Add the Worcestershire sauce and season to taste.
13. Serve the bobotie with this reduction and turmeric rice.

This recipe makes a mild bobotie. Adjust the curry powder according to taste. Serve with turmeric rice (see page 155).

Curried mince and
BABY CABBAGE PIE

SERVES 4

30 ml olive oil

10 ml Cape Malay curry
 powder

400 g baby cabbage,
 thinly sliced

7.5 ml salt

1 onion, chopped

2 cloves garlic, chopped

5 ml turmeric

500 g beef mince

freshly ground black pepper
 to taste

½ x 410 g can chopped
 tomatoes

5 ml sugar

125 ml water

15 ml Worcestershire sauce

400 g roll readymade
 puff pastry

1 egg

1. Preheat the oven to 200 °C on the thermo-fan setting.* Grease a large pie or 20 x 30 cm rectangular roasting dish.
2. Heat a large frying pan, add half the olive oil and half the curry powder and stir to release the flavour.
3. Add the cabbage and fry until tender, then season with 2.5 ml salt and spoon into the greased dish.
4. To the same pan, add the remaining olive oil and sauté the onion and garlic until softened.
5. Stir in the remaining curry powder and the turmeric, then add the mince and fry for 5–10 minutes until nearly dry and cooked.
6. Season with the remaining salt and some black pepper.
7. Add the tomatoes, sugar, water and Worcestershire sauce, and cook over medium heat until the liquid has reduced and thickened.
8. Spoon the mince mixture over the cabbage and mix lightly.
9. Roll out the pastry on a floured surface to 2 cm larger than your dish.
10. Roll the pastry over the rolling pin and unroll it over the pie filling and press it into the sides. Trim off any excess pastry with a sharp knife and make a few small incisions to allow steam to escape.
11. Beat the egg with 15 ml water and, using a pastry brush, brush the top of the pastry with the egg.
12. Bake for 20–30 minutes until golden.

* While a thermo-fan oven is preferable, a conventional oven will also work.

Cape Malay curry powder is very aromatic and complements this dish far better than plain curry powder.

Pure beef
BURGERS

BEEF PATTIES

500 g beef mince

30 ml Worcestershire sauce

15 ml tomato sauce

1 small onion, finely chopped

30 ml finely chopped
      fresh parsley

5 ml freshly ground
      black pepper

5 ml salt

olive oil to grill

ONIONS

15 ml olive oil

2 large onions, sliced
      into rings

SAUCE

60 ml mayonnaise

10 ml tomato sauce

10 ml chutney

TO SERVE

6 hamburger rolls

butter

lettuce leaves of your choice

sliced tomato

sliced cheese (optional)

1. Combine all the ingredients for the patties, except the olive oil, in a large bowl and mix well.
2. Using your hands, divide the mixture into six balls of approximately 80 g each.
3. Press them flat to form 1 cm thick patties.
4. Heat a griddle pan and, when hot, quickly brush with olive oil using a pastry brush.
5. Grill the patties on both sides until cooked to preference. Keep warm.
6. In a clean frying pan, heat the olive oil over low heat and fry the onions until soft.
7. To make the sauce, mix all the ingredients in a small bowl.
8. Halve and butter the rolls, then spread the bottom half of each roll with sauce.
9. Top the sauce with layers of lettuce and tomato, followed by a beef patty and onions.
10. Add a slice of cheese if desired before closing the burger with the top half of the roll.
11. Serve immediately.

To make mini burgers, simply make the patties a little smaller and use mini bread rolls (see the recipe on page 72).

Char-grilled
MARINATED RUMP STEAK

125 ml olive oil
60 ml Worcestershire sauce
50 g tomato paste
5 ml brown sugar
200–300 g rump steak per person
sea-salt flakes to taste

1. Place the olive oil, Worcestershire sauce, tomato paste and sugar in a jug and mix well.
2. Cut the rump steak into 200–300 g portions and place in a marinating bowl or other suitable container.
3. Pour over the marinade, seal with the lid and refrigerate for anywhere between 4 and 12 hours.
4. Preheat a griddle pan or heat a braai to the desired temperature.
5. Char-grill the steaks until cooked to preference.
6. With the last turn of the steak, season with sea-salt flakes.
7. Allow the meat to rest for 2 minutes before serving.

The marinade is enough for 1.5–2 kg steak and will keep in the fridge for up to seven days.

GRILLED STEAK
with parsley salt

250 ml fresh Italian parsley

10 ml sea salt flakes

freshly ground black pepper to taste

4 x 200 g matured sirloin or rump steaks

30 ml olive oil

1. On a wooden board, chop the parsley and mix with the salt and pepper. Spread the mixture over the entire board.
2. Preheat a griddle pan over high heat.
3. Brush both sides of each steak with olive oil and grill according to preference.
4. Place the grilled steaks onto the board covered with the parsley salt and rub the mixture in well on both sides.
5. Rest the steaks on the board for a few minutes before serving.

Serve these with any homemade steak sauce like monkey gland, cheese or mushroom. They pair particularly well with slow-baked creamy brown mushroom sauce (see page 311).

Slow-baked
BEEF SHORT RIBS

SERVES 4–6

15 ml olive oil

1 onion, sliced

1.2 kg beef short ribs, cut into
roughly 8 cm pieces

10 ml beef stock powder

500 ml water

10 ml salt

freshly ground black pepper
to taste

5 medium potatoes, peeled
and quartered

a few sprigs of fresh rosemary
to garnish

1. Preheat the oven to 180 ˚C.
2. Heat the olive oil in a large cast-iron or ovenproof saucepan with a lid over medium heat on the stovetop and sauté the onion until softened.
3. Add the short ribs and brown.
4. Mix the stock powder into the water and add to the pan. Season with half the salt and some black pepper.
5. Put on the lid and braise in the oven for 90 minutes.
6. After 90 minutes, add the potatoes and season them with the remaining salt.
7. Braise, covered, for another hour, then remove the lid and brown the meat in the oven, turning the ribs and potatoes a few times.
8. Garnish with fresh rosemary and serve immediately.

My kids call this 'Grandma's beef', because I told them my grandmother cooked this often for us when we were growing up. They've come to love this dish for its taste and my fond memories. Traditionally it is served with white rice, creamed green bean stew (see page 132) and caramelised cinnamon pumpkin (see page 131).

BEEF STROGANOFF

SERVES 4

15 ml olive oil

600 g matured rump steak,
    sliced into strips
    4 mm thick

5 ml salt

1 onion, finely diced

3 cloves garlic, chopped

300 g brown mushrooms,
    sliced 3 mm thick

5 ml paprika

30 ml cake flour

5 ml beef stock powder

250 ml water

60 ml sour cream

freshly ground black pepper
    to taste

fresh flat-leaf parsley
    to garnish

1. Heat a large frying pan with a lid over high heat and add the olive oil.
2. Brown the steak strips, season with the salt and set aside in a bowl along with the meat juices.
3. Turn down the heat to medium and sauté the onion in the same frying pan. Stir in the garlic, add the mushrooms and fry until cooked.
4. Return the steak and meat juices to the pan and sprinkle over the paprika and flour. Stir.
5. Dissolve the stock powder in the water and add to the pan.
6. Put on the lid and cook for 10 minutes until the liquid has reduced and thickened.
7. Add the sour cream and simmer for 5 minutes.
8. Season with black pepper and garnish with parsley before serving with long-grain white rice.

Red wine–infused BEEF PIE

SERVES 6–8

1.8 kg beef steak

30 ml olive oil

1 onion, diced

5 ml crushed garlic

leaves from a large sprig of
    fresh rosemary

10 ml salt

5 ml freshly ground
    black pepper

3 bay leaves

5 whole cloves

250 ml dry red wine

a knob of butter

400 g portabellini mushrooms,
    sliced

40 ml cake flour

5 ml beef stock powder

250 ml water

15 ml Worcestershire sauce

DOUGH

250 ml milk

250 ml sunflower oil

2 eggs

375 ml cake flour

20 ml baking powder

5 ml salt

1. Preheat the oven to 180 °C and grease a 25–30 cm round pie dish.
2. Lightly tenderise the steak with a meat mallet and cut into 2 cm cubes.
3. Heat the olive oil in a large cast-iron or ovenproof saucepan with a lid over medium heat on the stovetop and sauté the onion.
4. Add the garlic and steak and brown slightly.
5. Mix in the rosemary leaves, salt, pepper, bay leaves, cloves and wine.
6. Put on the lid and braise in the oven for 90 minutes or until the meat is tender.
7. Remove from the oven and turn up the heat to 200 °C.
8. Melt the butter in a large frying pan and sauté the mushrooms. Stir in the flour and then tip the mushrooms into the pan containing the meat. Mix well.
9. Mix the stock powder into the water and add this to the meat mixture along with the Worcestershire sauce.
10. Return the pan to the stovetop and simmer until the sauce has thickened, then spoon the mixture into the pie dish.
11. Place all the ingredients for the dough in a mixing bowl and whisk to form a runny dough.
12. Pour the dough over the pie filling, covering evenly.
13. Bake for 30 minutes until golden.

This pie has a soft pie dough that goes really well with the stewed red meat filling.

Tomato and OXTAIL STEW

SERVES 4–6

30 ml olive oil

1 onion, chopped

1 kg lean oxtail

750 ml water

10 ml beef stock powder

7.5 ml salt

2.5 ml freshly ground
  black pepper

10–12 baby potatoes, washed

½ x 410 g can chopped
  tomatoes

a sprig of fresh rosemary

350 g whole portabellini
  mushrooms

15 ml Worcestershire sauce

15 ml chutney

5–8 drops Tabasco® sauce

1. Preheat the oven to 180 °C.
2. Heat the olive oil in a large cast-iron or ovenproof saucepan with a lid over medium heat on the stovetop and sauté the onion.
3. Remove the onion and set aside in a small bowl.
4. In the same pan, brown the oxtail on all sides.
5. Return the onion to the pan and add the water, stock powder, salt and pepper.
6. Put on the lid and braise in the oven for 3 hours.* Make sure that the stock doesn't reduce completely during this time. Add another 250 ml water if necessary.
7. After 3 hours, add the potatoes, tomatoes and sprig of rosemary and braise, covered, for a further 2 hours.
8. Add the mushrooms, Worcestershire sauce, chutney and Tabasco® sauce and cook with the lid at a slight angle for another hour. The oxtail should be browned and the stock reduced enough to make a rich, thick gravy.
9. Remove the rosemary sprig and serve hot.

* If using a slow cooker, cook for at least 6–7 hours.

This is a wonderful winter dish. If you start preparing it at noon, the meal will be ready by early evening. Total cooking time is 5–6 hours. Although this stew takes a few hours to prepare, it is well worth the effort. Serve with rice or, my personal favourite with this stew, samp (see page 149).

LAMB CURRY

5 ml cumin seeds

5 ml coriander seeds

10 ml green cardamom pods

30 ml olive oil

1 large onion, chopped

10 ml crushed garlic

10 ml masala or medium
   curry powder

10 ml turmeric

10 ml ground cinnamon

5 ml ground ginger

1 kg cubed leg of lamb meat

410 g can chopped tomatoes

2–3 large potatoes, peeled
   and diced

10 ml salt

2.5–5 ml freshly ground
   black pepper

2 cinnamon sticks

4 bay leaves

10 ml sugar

30 ml fresh lemon juice

desiccated coconut and fresh
   parsley to garnish

chutney to serve

TOMATO SALSA

Mix the following:

½ onion, diced

2 large tomatoes, diced

60 ml chopped fresh parsley

salt and freshly ground black
   pepper to taste

1. In a small frying pan, dry-roast the cumin seeds, coriander seeds and cardamom pods for 2 minutes. Allow to cool and then grind in a mortar and pestle. Remove and discard the cardamom shells.

2. Heat half the olive oil in a large cast-iron saucepan with a lid and sauté the onion until softened.

3. Add the garlic and sauté for 1 minute.

4. Add the remaining olive oil and all the ground spices and sauté over medium heat for 1 minute.

5. Add the lamb, turn up the heat and fry for 5–10 minutes until just cooked.

6. Add the remaining ingredients, except the garnish, stir well, cover with the lid and simmer over low heat for 2–3 hours, until the lamb is tender. (Alternatively, bake in the oven on 180 ˚C for 2–3 hours.) Do not let the meat dry out – add a little water if necessary. The curry should make its own juices. Remove from the heat and rest for 30 minutes.

7. Gently warm the curry before garnishing with desiccated coconut and parsley and serving with rice, tomato salsa and chutney.

Lamb is ideal for curry because of its high fat content, which gives more flavour. If you can't find cubed leg of lamb, buy leg of lamb chops and cut the meat into cubes.

Lamb knuckle
POTJIE

SERVES 4–6

15 ml olive oil

1 onion, chopped

1 kg lamb knuckles

5 ml salt

freshly ground black pepper
   to taste

5 ml chicken stock powder

250 ml water

500 g baby potatoes, washed

300 g carrots, peeled and
   roughly chopped

200 g baby marrows, halved

a few sprigs of fresh rosemary
   to garnish

1. Preheat the oven to 180 ˚C.
2. Heat a large cast-iron or ovenproof saucepan with a lid on the stovetop, add the olive oil and sauté the onion until softened.
3. Add the lamb knuckles and brown on all sides. Season with the salt and some black pepper.
4. Mix the stock powder into the water and add to the pan.
5. Put on the lid and braise in the oven for 2–2½ hours until the meat is soft.
6. Add the potatoes and carrots and cook, covered, for 30 minutes.
7. Finally, add the baby marrows and cook, uncovered, for a further 30 minutes to reduce the stock and brown the meat.
8. Garnish with rosemary and serve with rice.

When cooked this way, the lamb knuckles will melt in your mouth.

LAMB LIVER AND KIDNEYS
with sweet and sour sauce

SERVES 4

MEALIE PAP

1.625 litres water

7.5 ml salt

500 ml good-quality mealie meal

100 g butter

SWEET AND SOUR SAUCE

375 ml water

10 ml chicken stock powder

10 ml Worcestershire sauce

30 ml brown sugar

30 ml white wine vinegar

30 ml cake flour

LAMB

500 g fresh lamb liver, trimmed
    and skinned

4 lamb kidneys, trimmed
    and skinned

juice of 1 lemon

5 ml salt

10 ml steak and chops spice

125 ml cake flour

30 ml olive oil

1 large onion, sliced

250 g rindless streaky
    bacon, diced

125 ml sunflower oil

freshly ground black pepper
    to taste

1. First put the mealie pap on to cook. Bring the water and salt to the boil in a medium saucepan with a lid. As the water starts to boil, add the mealie meal and briskly stir with a whisk until all the lumps have dissolved. (If the water is bubbling too vigorously, do not add the mealie meal. Remove the pan from the heat until the bubbling stops and then add the mealie meal.) Put on the lid, turn down the heat to low and cook for 30–45 minutes, stirring once or twice with a wooden spoon. Just before serving, add the butter and allow to melt. Stir through and serve hot.

2. To make the sauce, bring 250 ml of the water and all the other ingredients except the flour to the boil in a saucepan. Stir the flour into the remaining 125 ml water until combined and add to the saucepan, stirring continuously. Leave to simmer for 5 minutes. Keep warm.

3. For the lamb, cut the liver into 5 mm thick slices and slice the kidneys. Drizzle over the lemon juice and season with the salt and steak and chops spice.

4. Place the flour in a bowl, add the liver only and toss to coat.

5. Heat the olive oil in a large frying pan and sauté the onion until softened.

6. Add the bacon and kidneys and fry until the bacon is crispy.

7. In another large frying pan, heat the sunflower oil over medium heat and fry the floured liver in batches for 2 minutes on each side until cooked. Drain on paper towel.

8. Stir the liver into the kidney and bacon mixture and heat through.

9. Season with pepper and serve on the mealie pap, drenched in sweet and sour sauce.

LAMB SHANKS
slow cooked in red wine

SERVES 4

15 ml olive oil

1 onion, chopped

2 cloves garlic, chopped

4 lamb shanks

5 ml salt

freshly ground black pepper
    to taste

250 ml water

5 ml chicken stock powder

30 ml tomato paste

250 ml dry red wine

a large sprig of fresh rosemary

15 ml butter

1. Preheat the oven to 200 °C.
2. Heat the olive oil in a large cast-iron or ovenproof saucepan with a lid on the stovetop and sauté the onion until soft.
3. Add the garlic and sauté for a further minute.
4. Add the lamb shanks and brown on all sides. Season with the salt and some pepper.
5. Add the water, stock powder, tomato paste, wine and sprig of fresh rosemary.
6. Put on the lid and braise in the oven for 2½–3 hours until the stock has reduced and thickened and the shanks are tender. Check it every hour. If the stock has reduced too much, add another 250 ml water.
7. Just before serving, remove the rosemary sprig. Lift lamb shanks into a serving dish and stir the butter into the thickened stock.
8. Serve the lamb shanks on your starch of choice and spoon over the meat reduction.

Lamb shanks can be served with creamy mashed potatoes (see page 135), basmati rice (see page 145) or samp (see page 149).

Overnight
LEG OF LAMB

SERVES 8–10

30 ml olive oil

1 onion, roughly chopped

4–6 cloves garlic, chopped

2.5 kg leg of lamb

15 ml salt

5 ml freshly ground
  black pepper

100 ml Worcestershire sauce

2 sprigs fresh rosemary

3 bay leaves

10 ml whole cloves

500 ml water

6–8 medium potatoes

10–15 ml cake flour

1. The night before, preheat the oven to 125 °C.
2. Heat half the olive oil in a large cast-iron or ovenproof saucepan with a lid on the stovetop over medium heat and sauté the onion until soft.
3. Add the garlic and sauté for another minute.
4. Rub the leg of lamb with the remaining olive oil and the salt and pepper.
5. Place in the pan and sprinkle with Worcestershire sauce and cloves, add 1 rosemary sprig, the bay leaves and water.
6. Put on the lid and cook overnight (8–10 hours) in the oven.
7. The next morning, check that there is enough stock in the pan to cook the potatoes. If not, add more water.
8. Peel and quarter the potatoes and add to the meat. Turn up the oven to 160 °C and braise, covered, for another 4 hours. The lamb should be tender and grilled on top. If it has not grilled enough after 4 hours, tilt the lid slightly and cook for another 30 minutes. By now the potatoes should be browned and cooked through.
9. Remove the pan from the oven and let it rest for 10 minutes before transferring the contents to a serving dish. Leave 500 ml of the stock in the pan.
10. Deglaze the saucepan by reheating the reserved stock on the stovetop.
11. Mix the flour with 125 ml water, add to the pan and cook until the sauce has thickened. Season to taste and pour into a gravy boat.
12. Slice the meat and serve garnished with the remaining sprig of fresh rosemary and the reduction on the side.

This lamb is very tender and will fall off the bone. We have it for Sunday lunch with rice, butternut fritters (see page 141) and a green vegetable like creamed spinach (see page 134) or creamed green bean stew (see page 132).

Slow-baked salted
LAMB RIB

SERVES 4

1 lamb rib

10 ml salt

a few sprigs of fresh rosemary
to garnish

1. Preheat the oven to 180 °C.
2. Score the fat side of the rib into a diamond pattern.
3. Season the rib with salt on both sides and place on a drip tray in a roasting dish.
4. Bake, uncovered, for 3 hours until crispy, turning every 30 minutes.
5. Slice into portions and serve immediately, garnished with rosemary.

Crunchy and salty, this is by far one of my favourite ways to eat lamb rib. Serve with baby potatoes and vegetables or salad, or pap and tomato relish. I ask my butcher to cut the bones of the rib in half (at the back of the rib, leaving the meat intact in the front) to ensure the ribs are easy to portion and aren't too long.

Honey-glazed
GAMMON

1.5 kg wood-smoked gammon

2 carrots, quartered

1 onion, quartered

3 stalks celery, quartered

4 bay leaves

8 whole peppercorns

8 whole cloves

45 ml honey

**30 ml wholegrain Dijon
   mustard**

5 ml orange juice

100 g glacé cherries

toothpicks

1. Preheat the oven to 160 °C.

2. Place the gammon in a deep roasting dish together with the carrots, onion, celery, bay leaves, peppercorns and cloves. Add enough water to cover the meat.

3. Cover the dish with foil, shiny side down, and bake for 115 minutes (30 minutes for every 500 g, plus an additional 25 minutes).

4. Remove from the oven and transfer the gammon to a clean roasting dish. Discard the vegetables and meat juices.

5. Turn up the oven to 200 °C.

6. Remove and discard the skin from the gammon. Using a sharp knife, score the exposed fat in a diamond pattern.

7. Mix the honey, mustard and orange juice in a small bowl.

8. Press the cherries into the fat (one on each diamond) with toothpicks, covering the entire surface of the gammon.

9. Using a pastry brush, brush the cherries and exposed fat with the honey glaze.

10. Bake for 20 minutes until the fat is golden and crisp.

This gammon makes a wonderful Christmas dish and is beautiful served cold the next day. Serve with roast potatoes (see page 138) and sweet mustard (see page 304) or apple sauce.

Love: Love changes everything, overcomes anything; love remains forever.

CAKES, TARTS AND DESSERTS

I have found that most cakes taste best the day after baking. So to ensure optimal taste and satisfaction, always bake and decorate your cake a day in advance so that it can develop its flavour. When serving, set a glamorous table and make an occasion of it. I have used many of the cakes and tarts in this chapter as desserts and vice versa. Hot or cold, the desserts will tempt your taste buds and ensure that you end every meal on a high note.

CHOCOLATE CUPCAKES
with Nutella
buttercream icing

MAKES ABOUT 24

375 ml cake flour

310 ml white sugar

180 ml cocoa powder

7.5 ml bicarbonate of soda

5 ml baking powder

3 ml salt

180 ml buttermilk

60 ml sunflower oil

125 ml boiling water

5 ml vanilla essence

2 extra-large eggs

100 g hazelnuts, chopped

chocolate shapes to decorate

**NUTELLA BUTTERCREAM
    ICING**

250 ml soft butter

500 ml icing sugar, sifted

180 ml Nutella hazelnut
    chocolate spread

15 ml vanilla essence

about 60 ml cream

1. Preheat the oven to 180 °C and set the oven rack one above the middle. Line two 12-cup cupcake tins with cupcake liners.
2. Sift all the dry ingredients into a large mixing bowl.
3. Mix in the buttermilk, oil, water and vanilla essence with an electric mixer on low speed.
4. Add the eggs one at a time and mix until combined.
5. Spoon the batter into the cupcake liners until half full.
6. Bake for 20 minutes or until a cake tester or skewer inserted into the centre comes out clean.
7. Turn out onto a wire rack to cool.
8. To make the Nutella buttercream icing, cream the butter and icing sugar until pale and fluffy.
9. With the electric mixer running on low speed, add the Nutella and vanilla essence.
10. Increase to medium speed and add the cream, a tablespoon at a time, until the buttercream reaches the desired consistency. It should be light and fluffy.
11. Spoon the icing into a piping bag fitted with a large round nozzle.
12. Pipe a circle of icing around the outer edge of each cooled cupcake and sprinkle this with chopped hazelnuts.
13. Pipe a swirl of icing in the middle of the cupcake and decorate with a chocolate shape.

Laugh often
talk much
sit long

CUSTARD GATEAU
with maraschino cherries

MAKES 1 CAKE

6 extra-large eggs, separated

375 ml castor sugar

375 ml cake flour

100 ml cornflour

7.5 ml baking powder

2 ml salt

150 ml cold water

300 g maraschino cherries

CUSTARD

750 ml milk

125 ml custard powder

2 ml salt

200 g soft butter at room
   temperature

375 ml castor sugar

5 ml vanilla essence

1. Preheat the oven to 180 °C and grease two 24 cm spring-form cake tins.
2. In a large mixing bowl, beat the egg yolks and sugar until pale and fluffy.
3. Sift the flour, cornflour, baking powder and salt into another mixing bowl.
4. Add the cold water to the egg mixture.
5. With the electric mixer running on low speed, add the flour, a spoonful at a time, to the egg mixture until well combined.
6. In a separate bowl, beat the egg whites until stiff peaks form and then gently fold them into the batter.
7. Divide the batter between the cake tins and bake for 25–30 minutes until a cake tester or skewer inserted into the centre comes out clean.
8. Leave the cakes to stand in the tins for 5 minutes before turning out onto a wire rack to cool completely.
9. To make the custard, bring 500 ml of the milk to the boil in a saucepan.
10. Set a mixing bowl in a bowl of ice to chill.
11. Stir the custard powder and salt into the remaining milk and whisk this into the hot milk.
12. Keep stirring until the custard thickens, then turn down the heat to low and simmer for 3–4 minutes until the custard is cooked.
13. Pour the custard into the cold mixing bowl over ice and stir continuously with a whisk until the custard is completely cooled, ensuring there are no lumps. Pass through a sieve if necessary.
14. Cream the butter and sugar until pale and add the vanilla essence.
15. With the mixer on medium speed, add the custard, one spoonful at a time, to the sugar and butter mixture. Mix until smooth and all the custard has been incorporated.
16. Cut each cooled cake horizontally in two and divide the custard into five portions. Evenly spread a portion of custard over one layer of cake and stack another layer on top. Repeat the layers, using the last portion of custard to cover the whole cake, top and sides.
17. Decorate the top of the cake with the maraschino cherries.
18. Refrigerate the cake, removing it 30 minutes before serving.

Decadent
CARROT CAKE

MAKES 1 CAKE

432 g can pineapple crush

500 ml white sugar

4 extra-large eggs

5 ml vanilla essence

375 ml sunflower oil

5 ml bicarbonate of soda

15 ml milk

500 ml cake flour

5 ml baking powder

10 ml ground cinnamon

5 ml salt

750 ml coarsely grated carrot

200 g walnuts, chopped

ICING

500 g icing sugar, sifted

60 g soft butter

250 g tub smooth plain
   cream cheese

1. Preheat the oven to 180 ˚C and grease two 24 cm spring-form cake tins.
2. Strain the pineapple crush through a sieve and discard the juice.
3. Cream the sugar and eggs until pale and fluffy.
4. Add the vanilla essence.
5. With the electric mixer running on low speed, add the oil.
6. Mix the bicarbonate of soda into the milk and add to the batter.
7. Sift all the dry ingredients into a separate bowl.
8. With the mixer still on low speed, gradually add the dry ingredients.
9. Lastly, mix in the carrot, pineapple and 150 g of the walnuts.
10. Divide the batter between the cake tins and bake for about 1 hour until a cake tester or skewer inserted into the centre comes out clean.
11. Leave the cakes to stand in the tins for 5 minutes before turning out onto a wire rack to cool completely.
12. To make the icing, mix the icing sugar and butter until it resembles fine crumbs.
13. Add the cream cheese in batches, beating until light and fluffy. The consistency of cream cheese differs according to brand, so add just enough to make a soft but firm, spreadable icing.
14. Sandwich the cooled cakes together with a third of the icing and use the rest to ice the whole cake. Sprinkle over the remaining walnuts.

To develop its wonderful moist flavour, this cake should stand for a day before serving.

FRUIT CAKE

MAKES 1 CAKE

250 g blanched almonds,
　　chopped
500 g seedless raisins
500 g currants
500 g sultanas
125 g mixed citrus peel
125 g glacé cherries, quartered
625 g cake flour
500 g butter
375 g white sugar
10 extra-large eggs, whisked
30 g ground mixed spice
10 ml baking powder
5 ml bicarbonate of soda
15 ml hot water
375 ml sherry
375–500 ml whisky
marzipan and fondant icing to
　　decorate (optional)

1. Preheat the oven to 180 °C. Grease a 25 cm square or round cake tin and line with brown paper. The paper should stick out at least 7 cm above the rim of the tin. Grease the paper.
2. Roast the almonds on a large baking tray in the oven until golden brown.
3. Add all the fruit to the nuts on the baking tray and spread out evenly.
4. Return to the oven for 2–4 minutes until the fruit is heated through.
5. Sift 125 ml of the flour over the fruit and nuts and mix. Set aside.
6. Turn down the oven to 150 °C.
7. Cream the butter and sugar in an extra-large mixing bowl until pale.
8. Add the fruit mix and eggs to the butter and sugar mixture.
9. Sift over the remaining flour, the mixed spice and the baking powder.
10. Dissolve the bicarbonate of soda in the hot water and add to the mixture.
11. Add the sherry and mix well.
12. Pour the batter into the cake tin. It should be three-quarters full.
13. Bake for 1 hour, turn down the heat to 100 °C and bake for another 3½ hours until a cake tester or skewer inserted into the centre comes out clean.
14. Remove from the oven and leave in the tin for 5 minutes before turning out onto a wire rack to cool completely.
15. Drizzle the top of the cake with 125 ml whisky, flip it over and drizzle the bottom with another 125 ml. Wrap the cake in foil and place in an airtight container.
16. Drizzle 125 ml whisky over the cake after a week and leave it to ripen wrapped in foil in its airtight container for a maximum of three months. You can add another 125 ml whisky in this period if desired.
17. Serve as is or cover with marzipan and fondant icing.

This recipe is from my dear friend Marianne Hattingh's mother, Saartjie Spies of Ermelo. An old family favourite, it has been in their family for generations. It keeps for up to three months, so she usually bakes two, one to eat immediately and one to ripen for Christmas. She uses whisky only to cure it.

Honey and butter SPONGE CAKE

MAKES 1 CAKE

3 extra-large eggs
250 ml white sugar
375 ml cake flour
15 ml baking powder
a pinch of salt
125 g butter
250 ml milk
5 ml vanilla essence

HONEY SYRUP
45 ml butter
75 ml honey

1. Preheat the oven to 180 °C and spray a bundt tin with non-stick cooking spray.
2. In a large mixing bowl, cream the eggs and sugar until pale and fluffy.
3. Sift the flour, baking powder and salt into a separate bowl.
4. Heat the butter and milk together in a saucepan until the butter has melted.
5. Alternately add the milk and flour in batches to the egg mixture, mixing continuously until combined.
6. Add the vanilla essence.
7. Pour the batter into the cake tin and bake for 30 minutes until a cake tester or skewer inserted into the centre comes out clean.
8. Turn out the cake onto a serving plate.
9. Make the honey syrup by heating the butter and honey in a small saucepan until melted.
10. Pour the syrup over the cake and leave to cool.

I grew up with my mom serving this cake at teatime. I remember not being able to wait for it to cool completely, so we often ate it a little warm and it never lasted to the next teatime. This is best baked and enjoyed the same day.

MARMITE AND CHEESE CAKE

MAKES 1 CAKE

3 extra-large eggs
180 ml white sugar
375 ml cake flour
15 ml baking powder
a pinch of salt
125 g butter
180 ml milk
5 ml vanilla essence

TOPPING
45 ml Marmite
45 ml butter
500 ml grated Cheddar cheese

1. Preheat the oven to 180 °C and grease a 20 x 30 cm rectangular cake tin.
2. In a large mixing bowl, cream the eggs and sugar until pale and fluffy.
3. Sift the flour, baking powder and salt into a separate bowl.
4. Heat the butter and milk together in a saucepan until the butter has melted.
5. Alternately add the milk and flour in batches to the egg mixture, mixing continuously until combined.
6. Add the vanilla essence.
7. Pour the batter into the cake tin and bake for 25–30 minutes until a cake tester or skewer inserted into the centre comes out clean.
8. For the topping, heat the Marmite and butter in a small saucepan until melted.
9. Pour over the cake in the tin, spreading with the back of a spoon to cover the whole surface. Evenly sprinkle over the cheese and return to the oven to melt the cheese.
10. Remove from the oven and leave to cool before cutting into squares and serving.

This is for people who don't have a sweet tooth. The combination of sweet and salty in this recipe works perfectly. It is best baked and enjoyed the same day.

MOIST CHOCOLATE CAKE
with chocolate buttercream icing

MAKES 1 CAKE

375 ml cake flour

375 ml white sugar

90 ml cocoa powder

15 ml baking powder

a pinch of salt

180 ml boiling water

180 ml sunflower oil

6 extra-large eggs, separated

**CHOCOLATE BUTTERCREAM
   ICING**

325 g soft butter

750 g icing sugar, sifted

150 g cocoa powder, sifted

1. Preheat the oven to 180 °C and grease two 24 cm spring-form cake tins.
2. Sift all the dry ingredients together in a mixing bowl.
3. Add the boiling water and oil.
4. With the mixer running on medium speed, add the egg yolks one at a time.
5. In a separate large bowl, whisk the egg whites to soft peaks.
6. Fold the egg whites into the cake batter with a large metal spoon.
7. Divide the mixture between the two cake tins and bake for 20–25 minutes until a cake tester or skewer inserted into the centre comes out clean.
8. Leave the cakes in the tins for 10 minutes to cool and then turn out onto a wire rack to cool completely.
9. To make the icing, cream the butter with an electric mixer on medium speed until pale.
10. Add the icing sugar in batches and keep mixing until pale and fluffy.
11. With the mixer set on low speed, add the cocoa powder and beat until combined, light and fluffy. Do not overmix.
12. Place one of the cooled cakes on a cake plate and slightly trim the surface if it is too rounded.
13. Spread a third of the icing over the top in a thick layer and position the second cake on top.
14. Ice the whole cake, top and sides, with another third of the icing.
15. Spoon the remaining icing into a piping bag with the desired nozzle and decorate the cake.

This cake is really moist and is best enjoyed the day after baking.

Dark chocolate
GANACHE GATEAU

MAKES 1 CAKE

425 ml cake flour

310 ml white sugar

180 ml cocoa powder

5 ml baking powder

2.5 ml salt

250 ml buttermilk

125 ml sunflower oil

4 extra-large eggs

5 ml vanilla essence

10 ml bicarbonate of soda

180 ml hot black coffee

CHOCOLATE CREAM

90 g dark chocolate, chopped

590 ml cream

DARK CHOCOLATE
GANACHE

350 g dark chocolate, chopped

350 ml cream

125 g chocolate vermicelli
to decorate

125 g chocolate shavings
to decorate

1. Preheat the oven to 180 °C and grease two 24 cm spring-form cake tins.
2. Sift the flour, sugar, cocoa powder, baking powder and salt into a large mixing bowl and stir.
3. With an electric mixer on low speed, slowly add the buttermilk, oil, eggs and vanilla essence.
4. Mix the bicarbonate of soda into the coffee and add to the cake mixture. Mix to form a thin batter.
5. Pour the batter into the cake tins and bake for 35–40 minutes until a cake tester or skewer inserted into the centre comes out clean.
6. Allow the cakes to cool slightly in the cake tins before turning out onto a wire rack to cool completely.
7. Make the chocolate cream by melting 90 g chocolate in a bowl set over a saucepan of simmering water (the bowl must not touch the water).
8. Once melted, remove from the heat and stir in 90 ml of the cream. If the mixture solidifies, place it back over the simmering water and stir until smooth. Leave to cool slightly (it should still be pourable).
9. In a separate bowl and with an electric mixer, whisk the remaining cream to soft peaks.
10. Slowly pour the melted chocolate into the cream and, with the mixer on low speed, beat until the cream is whipped and thick. Do not overmix or the cream will separate.
11. Refrigerate for 15–20 minutes.
12. Slightly trim the surface of both cakes if they are too rounded. Place one of the cooled cakes on a disposable cake plate.
13. Spoon a quarter of the chocolate cream into a piping bag fitted with a 1 cm round nozzle and, starting in the middle and circling outwards, cover the top of the cake in a 1 cm thick layer of chocolate cream.
14. Position the second cake on top and cover the whole cake, top and sides, with two quarters of the chocolate cream. Smooth the top and sides with a flat cake knife or spatula.

15. Refrigerate the cake for at least 30 minutes. Keep the last quarter of chocolate cream in the fridge too.

16. To make the ganache, melt the chocolate in a bowl set over a saucepan of simmering water. Remove from the heat and stir in the cream until smooth. Leave to cool to room temperature (it should still be thin enough to pour).

17. Remove the cake from the fridge and place it on a wire rack set on a large baking tray.

18. Slowly pour the cooled chocolate ganache over the cold cake, carefully smoothing it out only if necessary with a flat cake knife or spatula, until the whole cake is covered. The excess ganache will drip onto the baking tray.

19. Pour the chocolate vermicelli into a bowl and, using a palette knife, press spoonfuls against the side of the cake, right around the bottom.

20. Refrigerate for at least 30 minutes until cold.

21. Remove the remaining chocolate cream from the fridge and spoon it into a piping bag fitted with a large star nozzle. Pipe rosettes around the top of the cake and sprinkle the chocolate shavings in the middle.

22. Keep the cake refrigerated until 30 minutes before serving.

This truly decadent showstopper is for the more experienced baker and should be baked with care and precision. It's best enjoyed the next day, so bake it a day in advance. Do yourself a favour and buy a thin, foil-covered, disposable cardboard cake plate the same size as your cake tins (available from most baking shops).

Red velvet CUPCAKES

MAKES 12

500 ml cake flour
310 ml white sugar
10 ml bicarbonate of soda
5 ml baking powder
2 ml salt
2 extra-large eggs
180 ml buttermilk
180 ml sunflower oil
60 ml beetroot juice
40 ml Crimson Pink
   food colouring
10 ml vinegar
5 ml vanilla essence

ICING
250 g icing sugar, sifted
30 g soft butter
60 ml smooth plain
   cream cheese

1. Preheat the oven to 180 °C and set the oven rack one above the middle. Line a 12-cup cupcake tin with cupcake liners.
2. Sift all the dry ingredients into a large mixing bowl.
3. Add the remaining ingredients and mix well with an electric mixer on medium speed.
4. Spoon the batter into the cupcake liners until three-quarters full.
5. Bake for 20 minutes until a cake tester or skewer inserted into the centre of a cupcake comes out clean.
6. Turn out the cupcakes onto a wire rack to cool.
7. In another mixing bowl, beat the icing sugar and butter until the mixture resembles coarse crumbs. Add the cream cheese, one spoon at a time, and mix well until pale and fluffy.
8. Spoon the icing into a piping bag with a star nozzle and ice the cupcakes.
9. Decorate as desired.

I would really recommend adding the beetroot juice (use an electric juicer to extract the juice from pieces of raw beetroot). It ensures that the cupcakes don't taste like food-coloured butter cake and adds to the red velvet colour.

APPLE TART

250 ml white sugar

2 extra-large eggs

250 ml cake flour

10 ml baking powder

a pinch of salt

180 ml milk

30 ml butter

385 g can pie apples

250 ml cream to serve

SAUCE

310 ml cream

160 ml white sugar

5 ml vanilla essence

1. Preheat the oven to 180 °C and grease a shallow 28 cm round pie dish.
2. Cream the sugar and eggs in a large mixing bowl until pale and fluffy.
3. Sift the dry ingredients into a separate bowl.
4. Heat the milk and butter in a saucepan until the butter has melted.
5. Add the milk and flour mixtures, a spoonful at a time, to the egg mixture and beat with an electric mixer on low speed until everything is combined.
6. Pour the batter into the pie dish.
7. Cut the pie apples slightly smaller and spread them over the batter.
8. Bake for 35–40 minutes until a cake tester or skewer inserted into the centre comes out clean.
9. While the tart is baking, pour the cream and sugar into a small saucepan and bring to boil. Turn down the heat to low and simmer for 5 minutes until thickened and then add the vanilla essence.
10. Remove the tart from the oven and pour over half of the sauce.
11. Return to the oven for another 5–10 minutes until golden brown on top.
12. Allow the tart to cool slightly before covering with the leftover sauce.
13. Serve warm with whipped cream.

Serve this as either a teatime treat or a dessert, accompanied by freshly whipped cream.

LEMON MERINGUE
pie

200 g packet Bakers Tennis® biscuits

90 ml butter

2 x 385 g cans condensed milk

6 extra-large eggs, separated

3–4 lemons

1.25 ml cream of tartar

250 ml castor sugar

1. Preheat the oven to 180 °C and grease a shallow 28 cm round pie dish.

2. Crush the biscuits in a mixing bowl and mix in the butter until it forms coarse crumbs.

3. Firmly press the biscuit crumbs into the pie dish, covering the base and sides.

4. Mix the condensed milk and egg yolks in a medium mixing bowl.

5. Squeeze one lemon at a time into the mixture (strain the lemon juice first to remove any pips) until you have achieved the desired taste.

6. Mix well, pour over the pie crust and bake for 10 minutes.

7. In the last 5 minutes of the baking time, in a separate bowl and using an electric mixer, whisk the egg whites and cream of tartar to soft peaks.

8. Turn the mixer to high speed and start adding the castor sugar, a third of the quantity at a time. Whisk until the meringue is thick and glossy.

9. Remove the pie from the oven and spoon over the meringue, covering the top.

10. Reduce the oven to 160 °C and bake the lemon meringue pie for another 15 minutes.

11. Turn off the oven and leave the lemon meringue pie inside to cool completely.

12. Refrigerate until ready to serve.

A lemon meringue pie should not be too sour, so taste the mixture every time you add lemon juice as each lemon contains different amounts of acidity and juice. Never use bottled lemon juice.

Old-fashioned
MILK TART

MAKES 1 TART

CRUST

250 ml cake flour

30 ml white sugar

5 ml baking powder

a pinch of salt

100 g cold butter

1 extra-large egg, whisked

CUSTARD

1.125 litres full-cream milk

100 g butter

1 cinnamon stick

3 extra-large eggs, separated

250 ml white sugar

125 ml cake flour

125 ml cornflour

a pinch of salt

seeds of 1 vanilla pod

15–30 ml ground cinnamon

1. Sift all the dry ingredients for the crust into a medium mixing bowl.
2. Grate the butter into the flour and mix with your fingertips or an electric mixer until it resembles coarse crumbs.
3. Add the whisked egg and mix until the dough is soft and pliable.
4. Bring the dough together into a ball, press it down into a disc and then wrap it in cling wrap. Rest the dough in the fridge for at least 30 minutes.
5. Preheat the oven to 180 °C and grease a shallow 28 cm round pie dish.
6. Using a rolling pin, roll out the dough on a floured surface until it is a little larger than the pie dish. Roll the dough over the rolling pin and unroll it over the pie dish.
7. With your fingertips, firmly press the dough into the bottom and sides of the dish. Cut off the excess dough with a knife. Line the pie shell with baking paper and fill with baking beans.
8. Blind bake the pastry for 15 minutes.
9. Remove from the oven and gently remove the paper and beans. Prick small holes in the pastry base with a fork, return to the oven and bake for another 10 minutes. Remove from the oven and allow to cool.
10. To make the custard, bring 1 litre of the milk, the butter and the cinnamon stick to the boil in a large saucepan. Remove and discard the cinnamon stick.
11. Mix the remaining 125 ml milk with the egg yolks, sugar, flour, cornflour and salt in a medium mixing bowl and then add to the milk in the saucepan. Whisk the custard over medium heat until smooth and thickened, then reduce the heat and simmer for 4–5 minutes until cooked. Remove from the heat.
12. Whisk the egg whites in a separate bowl until stiff peaks form. Fold the whites into the custard using a whisk until just combined.
13. Mix in the vanilla seeds and then pour the custard onto the pie crust. Dust the top with a thick layer of ground cinnamon and leave to set.

Strawberry YOGHURT TART

CRUST
200 g packet Bakers Tennis®
   biscuits
60 ml butter

FILLING
80 g packet strawberry
   jelly powder
125 ml boiling water
500 ml smooth strawberry
   yoghurt
385 g can condensed milk
250 ml cream, whipped
250 g fresh strawberries

1. Grease a loose-bottomed 24 cm cake tin with butter and line the bottom with baking paper, securing it when tightening the top part of the tin.
2. Crush the biscuits in a mixing bowl and mix in the butter until it forms coarse crumbs.
3. Firmly press the biscuit crumbs into the tin, covering the base and sides.
4. Dissolve the jelly powder in the boiling water in a medium mixing bowl.
5. Stir in the yoghurt and condensed milk and mix well.
6. Pour the filling onto the crust and spread out evenly.
7. Cover with cling wrap and refrigerate for 3–4 hours until set.
8. Gently remove the tart from the tin and decorate with whipped cream and strawberries.
9. Serve cold and refrigerate any leftovers.

This is a beautiful cold tart and a sure summer favourite. My children call it 'pink tart' because of its bright pink colour. Serve either at teatime or as a cold dessert.

PAVLOVA

6 extra-large egg whites

1 ml salt

2.5 ml cream of tartar

500 ml castor sugar

5 ml vanilla essence

360 g can caramel treat

250 ml cream

250 g fresh strawberries,
   hulled

1. Preheat the oven to 140 °C. Line a large baking tray with baking paper. Draw a circle 24 cm in diameter on a sheet of baking paper and spray with non-stick cooking spray.

2. In a large dry bowl, beat the egg whites, salt and cream of tartar with an electric mixer on medium speed until the mixture forms soft peaks.

3. Turn the mixer onto high speed and add the sugar in 4–6 parts, beating well after every addition. This takes about 10 minutes. The mixture should be thick, glossy and smooth.

4. Whisk in the vanilla essence.

5. Place a drop of meringue mixture underneath the four corners of the baking paper to secure it to the tray.

6. Spoon a third of the meringue onto the baking paper and spread it out to fill the drawn circle. Do not go over the lines.

7. Spoon the remaining meringue onto the outer edge of the circle, and use two spoons to shape it inwards and upwards, 6–7 cm high, like a volcano, leaving the middle hollow.

8. Bake for 20 minutes, then turn the oven to 120 °C and bake for another hour.

9. Turn off the oven, leaving the meringue inside until it has completely cooled.

10. Stir the caramel in the can until it is smooth and then spread it over the base of the meringue.

11. Beat the cream to stiff peaks and use to cover the caramel.

12. Arrange the strawberries on the cream.

13. Keep refrigerated and serve as a cake or cold dessert.

Named after the Russian ballerina Anna Pavlova, this dessert originated in Australia. It has a crusty outside and a soft centre and is traditionally decorated with fresh fruit and cream. Make sure to whisk the meringue until it is very stiff and thick, otherwise it will collapse and will not deliver on volume. The leftover egg yolks can be used to make custard or quiche.

Peppermint
CHOCOLATE TART

**200 g packet Bakers Tennis®
biscuits**
100 g butter
225 g peppermint chocolate
250 ml Orley Whip®
360 g can caramel treat

1. In a medium bowl, crush the biscuits into fine crumbs and add the butter.
2. Mix well until the mixture resembles coarse crumbs.
3. Grease a 20 x 30 cm rectangular pie dish with butter and cover the bottom with the crumbs, pressing down firmly to form a crust.
4. Divide the chocolate into two quantities: 150 g and 75 g.
5. Grate the chocolate, keeping it in two separate batches.
6. In a large mixing bowl, whip the Orley Whip® with an electric mixer until stiff.
7. With the mixer running on low speed, add the caramel, a spoon at a time, mixing until combined.
8. Using a large spoon, fold the 150 g grated chocolate into the thick cream mixture.
9. Spoon the filling onto the crust and spread it out evenly.
10. Sprinkle the 75 g grated chocolate over the filling.
11. Cover the tart with cling wrap and refrigerate for at least 3 hours before serving.
12. Refrigerate any leftovers.

Serve this tart as a tea-time treat or cold dessert.

TIRAMISU

SERVES 12

4 extra-large egg yolks

125 ml castor sugar

250 g mascarpone cheese

250 ml cream

90 ml Kahlua liqueur

30 ml instant coffee granules

500 ml warm water

200 g packet Italian ladyfingers
  (Savoiardi biscuits)

60 ml cocoa powder

1. Grease a 18 x 25 cm rectangular dish.
2. Place the egg yolks and sugar in a mixing bowl set over a saucepan of simmering water. The bowl should not touch the water.
3. With an electric mixer, beat the egg yolks and sugar until the mixture has tripled in volume and is thick and pale.
4. Remove the bowl from the heat and, using a whisk, fold in the mascarpone cheese until well combined.
5. In a separate bowl, whip the cream to stiff peaks.
6. Gently fold the Kahlua and then the cream into the egg mixture and refrigerate for at least 30 minutes.
7. Just before removing the mixture from the fridge, dissolve the coffee in the warm water in a medium bowl.
8. Quickly dip the biscuits one at a time into the coffee. Do not soak them!
9. Pack half the biscuits in rows into the bottom of the serving dish, evenly covering the base. You may need to cut some of the biscuits to fill any spaces.
10. Spoon half the filling onto the biscuits and spread it out evenly. Repeat the layers.
11. Using a fine sieve, sift the cocoa powder over the top until it is completely covered.
12. Refrigerate the tiramisu for at least 24 hours before cutting it into squares and serving.

This tiramisu is creamy and has a distinct liqueur taste. Make it a day in advance, as it is at its best the next day.

AFFOGATO

1 shot espresso (about 60 ml)
5 ml brown sugar
2–3 scoops vanilla ice cream
chocolate cigars to garnish

1. Make the espresso in a coffee machine or espresso pot.
2. Stir in the sugar and leave to cool slightly.
3. Place the ice-cream scoops in a parfait glass.
4. Pour the coffee over the ice cream and serve immediately, garnished with chocolate cigars.

An affogato is an Italian coffee-based beverage or dessert.

APPLE CRUMBLE

SERVES 6

2 x 385 g cans pie apples
5 ml ground cinnamon
125 ml cake flour
125 ml oats
125 ml brown sugar
80–100 g butter
125 ml flaked almonds
cream or ice cream to serve

1. Preheat the oven to 200 ˚C.
2. Grease a 28 cm round pie dish or six individual ramekins.
3. Cut the pie apples into thin slices and spread evenly over the base of the dish or divide between the ramekins.
4. Sprinkle the apples with cinnamon.
5. Mix the flour, oats and sugar in a large bowl.
6. Melt the butter in a small saucepan, pour over the flour mixture and mix until crumbly.
7. Spoon the crumble over the apples, ensuring all the apples are covered.
8. Sprinkle over the flaked almonds and bake for 20–25 minutes until golden brown.

This is best served warm with cream or ice cream.

APPLE STRUDEL

SERVES 8–10

DOUGH
700 ml cake flour
200 ml water
125 ml sunflower oil
5 ml salt

FILLING
10 Granny Smith apples,
    peeled and cored
120 g butter
125 ml brown sugar
5 ml ground cinnamon
5 ml ground allspice
125 ml seedless raisins

SAUCE
125 g butter
125 ml white sugar
100 ml cream
100 ml milk
5 ml ground cinnamon
5 ml ground allspice

cream or ice cream to serve

1. Place all the ingredients for the dough in a mixer and mix for 10 minutes until the dough is soft and smooth. Cover with cling wrap and let it rest in a warm place for 3–4 hours.
2. Preheat the oven to 200 ˚C and grease a baking tray.
3. Cut the apples into 3–4 mm slices and place them in a medium mixing bowl.
4. Melt the butter in a small saucepan and stir in the sugar and spices until the sugar has dissolved.
5. Gently mix the melted butter into the apples. The butter mixture will become grainy.
6. Add the raisins and mix.
7. Using a rolling pin, roll out the dough on a floured surface into a paper-thin, 45 x 55 cm rectangle. Position the rectangle with the short edge facing you.
8. Evenly spread the apples over the dough, leaving a 5 cm border on all sides.
9. Fold over the top 5 cm of dough and roll once with the apples, like a Swiss roll.
10. Fold over the 5 cm of dough on the left and right sides.
11. Now roll the dough towards you until it is neatly rolled up into a loaf.
12. Carefully place the strudel on the baking tray and, with a knife, make slits in the dough to allow steam to escape.
13. Bake for 45 minutes.
14. While the strudel is baking, caramelise the butter and sugar over low heat in a small saucepan. Add the cream and milk and stir until any lumps have dissolved. Add the spices and cook the sauce for 2 minutes.
15. Serve the strudel warm with the spicy caramel sauce and a dollop of cream or ice cream.

Chocolate
BROWNIES

150 g butter
125 g dark chocolate, chopped
250 ml white sugar
a pinch of salt
3 extra-large eggs, separated
125 ml cake flour
45 ml cocoa powder
2.5 ml baking powder
100 g pecan nuts, coarsely
   chopped
sifted icing sugar to serve
cream or ice cream to serve

1. Preheat the oven to 150 ˚C and grease a 20 cm square cake or brownie tin.
2. Melt the butter and chocolate together in a medium bowl placed over a small saucepan of simmering water. Make sure that the bowl does not touch the water.
3. Remove the bowl from the heat and mix the sugar and salt into the chocolate mixture.
4. Using a whisk, mix the egg yolks into the chocolate mixture, one yolk at a time.
5. Sift the flour, cocoa powder and baking powder together in a separate bowl, and then fold this into the chocolate mixture.
6. In another medium bowl, whisk the egg whites into soft peaks and then fold into the mixture.
7. Finally, fold in the chopped pecans.
8. Spoon the mixture into the cake tin and level the top.
9. Bake for 45 minutes and then remove from the oven.
10. Allow the brownies to set for a few minutes before cutting into squares in the tin.
11. Dust with icing sugar and serve warm, either plain or with cream or ice cream.

Chocolate MOUSSE

SERVES 6–8

150 g good-quality dark
   chocolate, chopped
4 extra-large eggs, separated
45 g castor sugar
15 ml cocoa powder
150 ml cream
a pinch of salt

1. Place the chocolate in a bowl over a saucepan of simmering water, making sure that the bowl does not touch the water. Slowly melt the chocolate, stirring every now and then.
2. Once the chocolate has melted, turn off the heat but keep the bowl over the hot water.
3. In a separate bowl, use an electric mixer to whisk the egg yolks and sugar until pale and fluffy.
4. Sift in the cocoa powder and mix well.
5. Slowly add the egg-yolk mixture to the melted chocolate in the bowl over the hot water and mix until smooth. Remove from the heat and allow the mixture to cool slightly.
6. In another bowl, whisk the cream until it forms soft peaks.
7. Whisk a spoonful of this whipped cream into the chocolate mixture until smooth.
8. Using a metal spoon, gently fold the rest of the cream into the mixture, taking care to not mix too much.
9. In a separate bowl, use an electric mixer to whisk the egg whites with a pinch of salt to soft peaks.
10. Gently fold the egg whites into the chocolate mixture, retaining the volume.
11. Spoon the mousse into ramekins or glasses and chill in the fridge for at least 2 hours.
12. Decorate as desired.

CHOCOLATE PRALINE MERINGUE
with cherries and berries

SERVES 10–12

175 g whole almonds

200 g castor sugar

200 g brown sugar

50 g demerara sugar

6 extra-large egg whites

10 ml white wine vinegar

45 ml cocoa powder

TOPPING

90 g dark chocolate, chopped

30 ml milk

360 g can caramel treat

250 ml cream

200 g fresh cherries

120 g fresh blueberries

100 g fresh mulberries
  or blackberries

1. Preheat the oven to 140 °C. Line a large baking tray with baking paper and spray with non-stick cooking spray.
2. Toast the almonds in a dry frying pan over medium heat and allow to cool completely. Roughly chop the almonds to make coarse crumbs.
3. Combine the three varieties of sugar in a medium mixing bowl.
4. In a large bowl, beat the egg whites on medium speed until they start to thicken, then turn the speed to high and beat until stiff peaks form.
5. Add the sugar, 150 g at a time, beating well after each addition. This takes 8–10 minutes. The mixture should be thick, glossy and heavy.
6. Add the vinegar, sift in the cocoa powder and mix well.
7. Fold in the chopped almonds.
8. Place a drop of meringue mixture underneath the four corners of the baking paper to secure it to the tray.
9. Spoon the mixture onto the baking paper and form a circle. Depending on the size of the baking tray, you can make one 35–40 cm circle or two 24 cm circles using two baking trays. The meringue will spread another 2–3 cm while baking.
10. Bake for 1 hour. Turn off the oven and leave the meringue inside to cool.
11. Melt the chocolate with the milk in a bowl over a saucepan of simmering water, making sure that the bowl does not touch the water. Remove from the heat, stir until smooth and set aside.
12. Place the meringue on a large plate and spread the caramel on top.
13. Whip the cream to stiff peaks and spoon over the caramel.
14. Cover the surface with the cherries and berries and drizzle over the chocolate sauce. Keep any leftovers in the fridge.

This festive, sumptuous dessert is perfect for the holiday season.

CHOCOLATE SOUFFLÉ TART
with raspberries

SERVES 8–10

90 g dark chocolate, chopped

125 ml cocoa powder, sifted

250 ml castor sugar

150 ml boiling water

2 egg yolks

75 ml ground almonds

45 ml cake flour, sifted

4 egg whites

2.5 ml cream of tartar

60 ml icing sugar

200 g fresh raspberries

whipped cream to serve

1. Preheat the oven to 190 °C and grease a 28 cm loose-bottomed quiche tin.
2. Combine the chocolate, cocoa powder and 125 ml of the castor sugar in a mixing bowl.
3. Add the boiling water and stir until smooth and the chocolate has melted.
4. Stir in the egg yolks, followed by the ground almonds and flour.
5. In a separate bowl, use an electric mixer on medium speed to whisk the egg whites and cream of tartar to soft peaks. Then turn the mixer to high speed, add the remaining castor sugar and whisk until thick and glossy.
6. Fold the egg-white mixture into the chocolate mixture.
7. Pour the batter into the prepared tin and bake for 35–40 minutes until puffed and set.
8. Gently lift the tart from the tin and place it on a serving plate.
9. Dust the tart with the icing sugar and decorate with raspberries. Serve warm with whipped cream.

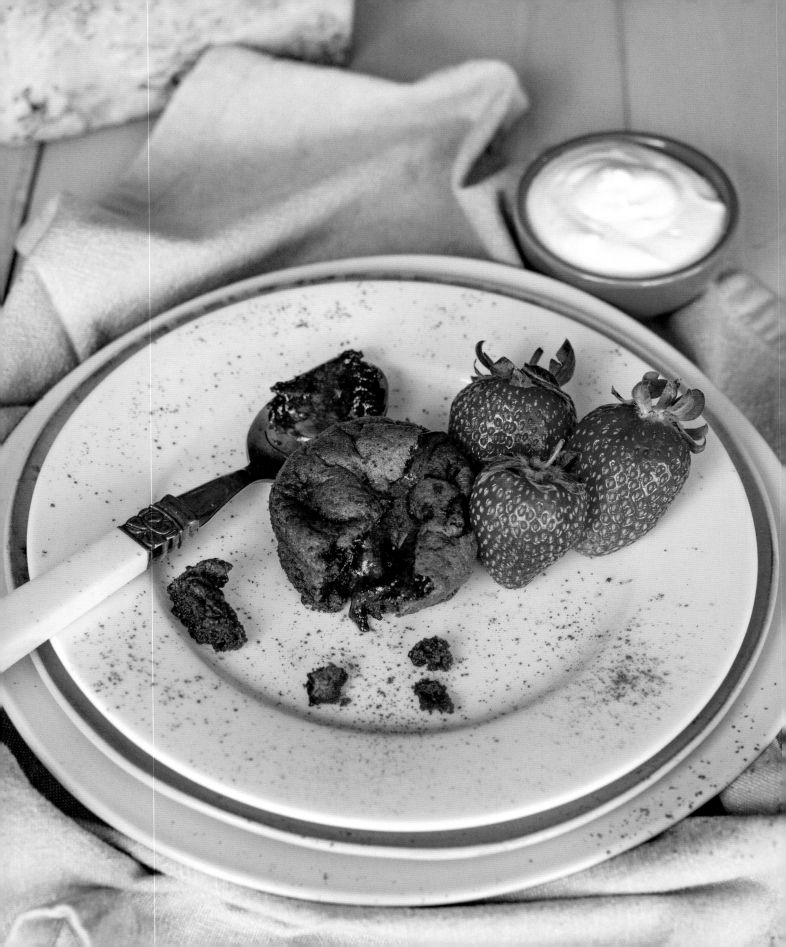

Chocolate VOLCANOES

SERVES 10–12

150 g dark chocolate, chopped

150 g butter

3 extra-large eggs

3 egg yolks

100 ml castor sugar

80 ml cake flour, sifted

fresh berries and cream or
    ice cream to serve

1. Preheat the oven to 200 ˚C and grease two muffin tins well.
2. Melt the chocolate and butter in a medium bowl set over a small saucepan of simmering water and stir until smooth.
3. Remove from the heat and leave to cool slightly.
4. In a separate large bowl, beat the eggs, egg yolks and sugar until pale and fluffy.
5. Add the chocolate mixture to the egg mixture and mix well.
6. Gently fold in the sifted flour.
7. Spoon the mixture into the muffin tins, filling each hole to three-quarters full.
8. Bake on the middle rack of the oven for 12–14 minutes. The puddings should be cooked on the outside but still runny in the middle. The puddings will start to rise just before they are ready.
9. Remove from the oven and gently lift out each pudding with a spoon and place on individual serving plates. Serve immediately with fresh berries and cream or ice cream.

My son Lou named these puddings 'chocolate volcanoes' because they ooze with gooey chocolatey custard. Because this recipe is sensitive to oven temperatures, do a test batch to see exactly how long your oven takes to cook them to perfection. They can also be baked in small ramekins.

Cinnamon
DUMPLINGS

SAUCE

875 ml water

250 ml white sugar

15 ml butter

5 ml ground cinnamon

a pinch of salt

DOUGH

310 ml cake flour

5 ml baking powder

a pinch of salt

125 ml white sugar

60 ml butter

1 extra-large egg

60 ml cold water

warm vanilla custard to serve

1. Make the sauce first. Place all the ingredients in a large saucepan, put on the lid and bring to the boil, then turn down the heat to low.
2. Sift the cake flour, baking powder, salt and sugar into a large mixing bowl. Sift once more (this is very important).
3. With a fork, work the butter into the flour until the mixture resembles breadcrumbs.
4. Whisk the egg and cold water together in a separate bowl and then add to the mixture. Stir until well combined.
5. Place tablespoonfuls of dough into the simmering syrup as quickly as possible and put on the lid.
6. Simmer and steam for at least 10 minutes without taking off the lid.
7. Spoon the dumplings and sauce into a serving dish and serve immediately with warm custard.

Butter and cinnamon CRÊPES

MAKES 15

250 ml cake flour

250 ml water

250 ml milk

1 extra-large egg

15 ml sunflower oil, plus extra to cook

2.5 ml lemon juice

2.5 ml baking powder

1 ml salt

200 ml white sugar mixed with 50 ml ground cinnamon

butter to serve

lemon wedges to serve

1. Place all the ingredients up to and including the salt into a mixing bowl.
2. Beat with an electric hand mixer until well combined.
3. Cover the bowl with cling wrap and rest for 30 minutes.
4. When ready to cook, heat 2.5 ml sunflower oil in an 18 cm frying pan. The oil must be hot; if it is not, the first two crêpes will stick to the pan.
5. Pour just enough batter into the pan to thinly coat the bottom.
6. Cook until the batter is light brown underneath, then turn over the crêpe and seal the other side for about 10 seconds.
7. Slip the crêpe onto a plate, cover with cinnamon sugar and place a dot of butter in the middle.
8. Roll up and serve immediately with lemon wedges on the side.

French crêpes are a little thinner than our local pancakes. These buttery ones are best served straight from the pan. You will never use another pancake recipe again!

CRÊPES SUZETTE

SERVES 5–8

a batch of butter and cinnamon crêpes (see opposite page)
250 ml freshly squeezed orange juice
125 ml white sugar
50 ml water
15 ml cornflour
a pinch of salt
grated rind of 1 orange
vanilla ice cream and orange slices to serve

1. Cook the crêpes one by one, stacking them up on a plate as you go. Cover the plate with cling wrap to keep the crêpes moist.
2. Place the orange juice, sugar, water, cornflour and salt into a small saucepan and simmer for 5 minutes, stirring to dissolve the sugar. You can use the syrup straight away, or allow it to cool and simply reheat before serving.
3. Fold the crêpes in half, and then in half again to resemble a fan.
4. Arrange two or three crêpes on each serving plate, cover them in the warm syrup and garnish with grated orange rind. Serve with scoops of ice cream and slices of orange.

Date and nut
BRANDIED PUDDINGS

SERVES 10

125 g pitted dates, finely
   chopped

250 ml hot water

5 ml bicarbonate of soda

150 ml brown sugar

30 ml butter

a pinch of salt

1 extra-large egg

5 ml baking powder

310 ml cake flour

125 ml chopped pecan nuts

SYRUP

375 ml cream

60 g butter

125 ml brown sugar

5 ml brandy

5 ml vanilla essence

1. Preheat the oven to 180 °C and set the oven rack one above the middle. Grease 2 x 6-cup muffin tins.
2. Place the dates in a medium mixing bowl and add the hot water, bicarbonate of soda, sugar, butter and salt. Let the mixture stand for 10 minutes.
3. Beat in the egg, then sift in the baking powder and flour and mix well.
4. Stir in the pecan nuts.
5. Spoon the mixture into the muffin tins, filling each hole to three-quarters full.
6. Bake for 20 minutes until a cake tester or skewer inserted into the centre of a muffin comes out clean.
7. While the puddings are baking, make the sauce. Place 125 ml of the cream along with the butter and sugar into a small saucepan and bring to the boil.
8. Turn down the heat to low and cook for 5 minutes. Turn off the heat and stir in the brandy and vanilla essence.
9. Whip the remaining cream in a separate bowl.
10. Plate each pudding and pour over the hot syrup just before serving.
11. Serve with a dollop of whipped cream.

You can serve these individual puddings without the sauce for an equally decadent muffin.

Festive
ICE-CREAM CAKE

SERVES 10–12

2 litres vanilla ice cream,
 slightly thawed
100 g red glacé cherries
100 g pecan nuts, roughly
 chopped
360 g can caramel treat
2 litres chocolate ice cream,
 slightly thawed
40 g Cadbury Crunchie®
 chocolate bar, cut into
 1 cm pieces
250 ml chocolate chips
200 g packet Bakers
 Choc-kits® biscuits
200 g milk chocolate, chopped
125 g chocolate malted puffs
32 g Cadbury Flake®
 chocolate bar

1. Line a 12 x 30 cm loaf tin with cling wrap.
2. Place the vanilla ice cream into a large mixing bowl.
3. Halve three-quarters of the cherries, leaving the remainder whole.
4. Mix the chopped cherries and pecan nuts into the vanilla ice cream.
5. Spoon the mixture into the loaf tin and press down evenly.
6. Place in the freezer for 10 minutes.
7. Stir the caramel in the can and then spoon a layer onto the ice-cream mixture.
8. Freeze for another 10 minutes.
9. Place the chocolate ice cream into a large, clean mixing bowl.
10. Mix the Crunchie® and chocolate chips into the chocolate ice cream.
11. Spoon the chocolate ice-cream mixture into the loaf tin, press down evenly, and top with another layer of caramel, being sure to leave enough room for a layer of biscuits.
12. Freeze for another 10 minutes.
13. Roughly crush the Choc-kits® into coarse crumbs and evenly spread over the top of the ice-cream cake. Press down firmly with a spatula or egg lifter and cover the tin with cling wrap.
14. Return to the freezer until completely frozen.
15. Melt the milk chocolate in a bowl set over a small saucepan of simmering water. Allow to cool slightly.
16. Remove the tin from the freezer and unwrap the cling wrap. Gently turn out the ice-cream cake onto a large rectangular serving plate and remove the cling wrap from the base.
17. Drizzle the slightly cooled chocolate over the cake and decorate with the whole glacé cherries and chocolate malted puffs. Crumble the Flake® over the top.
18. Freeze for 5 minutes before serving.
19. Cut into 1-cm-thick slices and serve.

WAFFLES

410 ml cake flour

30 ml castor sugar

15 ml baking powder

a pinch of salt

310 ml milk

40 g butter, melted

3 extra-large eggs, separated

vanilla ice cream and honey/golden syrup to serve

1. Preheat the oven to 160 ˚C.
2. Sift all the dry ingredients into a large mixing bowl.
3. Mix the milk, melted butter and egg yolks in a separate bowl and add to the dry ingredients. Mix well.
4. In another bowl, whisk the egg whites to stiff peaks and then fold into the batter.
5. Heat a waffle pan over high heat (or use an electric waffle iron) and spray with non-stick cooking spray.
6. Spoon the batter into the waffle pan and cook for 3–4 minutes until golden brown.
7. Keep the cooked waffles in the oven on a wire rack while you cook the rest to ensure that they stay crispy.
8. Serve the warm waffles topped with dollops of ice cream and drizzled with honey or golden syrup.

ICE CREAM
and chocolate sauce

250 g milk chocolate, chopped

250 ml cream

ice cream to serve

1. Gently melt the chocolate in a medium bowl set over a small saucepan of simmering water.
2. Once melted, stir in the cream until completely mixed.
3. Pour the sauce into a jug and serve with your favourite ice cream.

I like to serve my ice cream and chocolate sauce in pretty glasses and decorated with glacé cherries and chopped nuts.

Hope: Hope gives us courage for today and vision for tomorrow.

RUSKS, BISCUITS AND SWEETS

I always have rusks and biscuits in my kitchen, stored in glass containers for all to see. Rusks make a great snack with coffee or tea in the early morning or late afternoon when you feel peckish. I love having a biscuit or sweet treat with a cup of tea mid-morning. We hardly ever buy these, as I like baking them. Come the end of November, we usually bake cake tins full of rusks, biscuits and sweet treats to take away on holiday with us. My children, who study away from home, love having rusks and coffee while studying, so they usually put in orders the week before they come home.

Buttermilk RUSKS

2.35 kg cake flour

750 ml white sugar

30 ml baking powder

40 ml cream of tartar

10 ml salt

1 kg cold butter

5 extra-large eggs

250 ml cream

2 x 500 g buttermilk

10 ml bicarbonate of soda

1. Sift the flour, sugar, baking powder, cream of tartar and salt into an extra-large mixing bowl.
2. Grate over the butter and work it in by hand until there are no lumps.
3. Beat the eggs, cream and buttermilk in a separate large bowl.
4. Mix the bicarbonate of soda with 15 ml hot water and add to the egg mixture.
5. Add the egg mixture to the flour mixture and mix well.
6. Knead for 15–20 minutes to form a soft dough. If you have a standing electric mixer, you can knead the dough in three to four batches – it will be quicker.
7. Preheat the oven to 180 ˚C on the thermo-fan setting* and spray 3–4 large (35 x 15 cm) loaf tins with non-stick cooking spray.
8. Pinch off golf-ball-sized balls of dough and form them into fingers, 4–5 cm long.
9. Pack them standing up in rows in the loaf tins.
10. Bake for 80 minutes until cooked. A cake tester or skewer inserted into the centre of a rusk should come out clean.
11. Remove from the tins and leave the rusks to cool completely on a wire rack.
12. Heat the oven to 50 ˚C on the thermo-fan setting.
13. Cut or break the rusks into fingers, place on baking trays and dry overnight in the oven.
14. Store in airtight containers.

* While a thermo-fan oven is preferable, a conventional oven will also work.

This recipe is an old family favourite from my dear friend Lynette Steyn Laurens's mother, Elza Robinson.

Muesli
RUSKS

1 kg self-raising flour
500 g nutty wheat flour
300 g Kellogg's All-Bran®
flakes
1 kg muesli with raisins
and nuts
560 g brown sugar
30 ml baking powder
5 ml salt
300 g sunflower seeds
100 g sesame seeds
100 g linseeds
4 extra-large eggs
5 ml bicarbonate of soda
500 g butter
3 x 500 g buttermilk

1. Preheat the oven to 180 °C on the thermo-fan setting* and spray two 35 x 15 cm loaf tins with non-stick cooking spray.
2. Sift the flour into an extra-large mixing bowl and add all the dry ingredients, except the bicarbonate of soda. Mix well.
3. Whisk the eggs in a separate bowl and add the bicarbonate of soda.
4. Melt the butter in the microwave oven and mix into the eggs along with the buttermilk.
5. Make a hole in the middle of the dry ingredients and pour the liquid into it.
6. Mix well with a wooden spoon.
7. Divide the batter between the loaf tins and smooth the tops evenly with a fork.
8. Bake for 90 minutes until cooked. A cake tester or skewer inserted into the centre should come out clean.
9. Remove from the tins and leave the rusks to cool completely on a wire rack.
10. Heat the oven to 50 °C on the thermo-fan setting.
11. Cut the rusks into fingers (I have found that an electric carving knife works really well and doesn't break the rusks), place on baking trays and dry overnight in the oven.
12. Store in airtight containers.

* While a thermo-fan oven is preferable, a conventional oven will also work.

I have developed this recipe over the years and it's proved to be a winner. These rusks are healthy and filling, and full of seeds, nuts and raisins. Once dipped in coffee, they crumble in your mouth. Oven temperatures differ. Overnight drying can vary between 50 °C and 100 °C.

Old-fashioned ANISEED RUSKS

MAKES ABOUT 190

250 g butter
500 ml warm boiled water
500 ml cold water
625 ml white sugar
50 g fresh yeast
625 ml cake flour
2 extra-large eggs, whisked
½ x 385 g can condensed milk
20 ml salt
20 ml aniseed
about 3.25 litres cake flour

SUGAR SYRUP
45 ml white sugar
125 ml boiling water

1. In an extra-large mixing bowl, melt the butter in the warm boiled water and then stir in the cold water and sugar.
2. Add just enough water to the yeast to dissolve it.
3. Mix the yeast and the 625 ml flour into the butter mixture and leave to stand for 10 minutes.
4. Stir in the eggs, condensed milk, salt and aniseed.
5. Start adding the 3.25 litres of flour a cup at a time, mixing after every addition, until you have a soft dough. Knead for 15–20 minutes.
6. Cover with cling wrap and place the bowl in a clean plastic bag. Leave in a warm spot for about 4 hours to prove until doubled in size.
7. Spray three 35 x 15 cm loaf tins with non-stick cooking spray.
8. Pinch off golf-ball-sized balls of dough and form them into fingers, 7 cm long.
9. Pack them standing up in rows in the loaf tins. You should get 4 rows of 16 per tin.
10. Cover with cling wrap and leave to prove for about 2 hours until doubled in size. The dough should not rise over the sides of the tins.
11. Preheat the oven to 160 °C and bake the rusks for 1 hour.
12. Remove from the oven and turn out the 'loaves' onto a wire cooling rack.
13. Make the sugar syrup by dissolving the sugar in the boiling water. Using a pastry brush, paint the tops and sides of the loaves.
14. Eat warm or leave to cool, break into rusks and dry overnight on baking trays in a 50 °C oven.
15. Store in airtight containers.

This is my sister-in-law Madeleine van Blerk's recipe. We love eating these rusks warm, straight from the oven, so the first tin never lasts to be dried later. Wrap a loaf in cling wrap and it will keep fresh for a few days. The rest of the rusks can be dried overnight and kept for weeks in airtight containers.

Almond
BISCOTTI

MAKES ABOUT 1 KG (60–70)

100 g butter

375 ml brown sugar

3 extra-large eggs

750 ml cake flour

15 ml baking powder

180 ml cornflour

100 g raw almonds, chopped

1 ml almond essence

1. Preheat the oven to 180 °C and place the oven rack one above the middle. Spray a large baking tray with non-stick cooking spray.
2. Cream the butter and sugar until pale and fluffy, using an electric mixer.
3. Add the eggs one at a time, beating after each addition.
4. Sift the flour, baking powder and cornflour together in a separate bowl.
5. With the mixer running on low speed, add the flour in batches to the egg mixture. Lastly add the nuts and almond essence.
6. Turn out the dough onto a floured surface and divide in half.
7. Roll each half into a roll, 30–35 cm long.
8. Place the rolls next to each other on the greased baking tray, leaving space between them. Press each roll flat to about 3 cm thick and 5 cm wide.
9. Bake for 25 minutes.
10. Remove from the oven and leave to cool.
11. Heat the oven to 50 °C on the thermo-fan setting.*
12. Carefully cut each roll into 1-cm-thick slices on a wooden board.
13. Place the slices flat on large baking trays and dry in the oven for 5 hours.
14. Store in airtight containers.

* While a thermo-fan oven is preferable, a conventional oven will also work.

Biscotti, meaning 'twice baked', are beautiful Italian biscuits that can be enjoyed with tea or coffee.

Chocolate
BISCOTTI

MAKES ABOUT 1 KG (60–70)

150 g blanched almonds

100 g butter

375 ml brown sugar

3 extra-large eggs

20 ml strong coffee

750 ml cake flour

15 ml baking powder

180 ml cocoa powder

100 g dried cranberries,
    chopped

1. Preheat the oven to 180 ˚C and place the oven rack one above the middle. Spray a large baking tray with non-stick cooking spray.
2. Toast the almonds in a dry frying pan over medium heat and then roughly chop.
3. Cream the butter and sugar until pale and fluffy, using an electric mixer.
4. Add the eggs one at a time, beating after each addition.
5. Stir in the coffee.
6. Sift the flour, baking powder and cocoa powder together in a separate bowl.
7. With the mixer running on low speed, add the flour in batches to the egg mixture. Lastly add the nuts and cranberries.
8. Turn out the dough onto a floured surface and divide in half.
9. Roll each half into a roll, 30–35 cm long.
10. Place the rolls next to each other on the greased baking tray, leaving space between them. Press each roll flat to about 3 cm thick and 5 cm wide.
11. Bake for 25 minutes.
12. Remove from the oven and leave to cool.
13. Heat the oven to 50 ˚C on the thermo-fan setting.*
14. Carefully cut each roll into 1 cm thick slices on a wooden board.
15. Place the slices flat on large baking trays and dry in the oven for 5 hours.
16. Store in airtight containers.

* While a thermo-fan oven is preferable, a conventional oven will also work.

Chocolate
MERINGUES

MAKES 50–60

4 egg whites
375 ml castor sugar
10 ml white vinegar
45 ml cocoa powder, sifted
90 g chocolate chips (optional)

1. Preheat the oven to 125 °C and spray a large baking tray with non-stick cooking spray.
2. Using an electric mixer, whisk the egg whites on medium speed until frothy.
3. Increase the speed to high and whisk until soft peaks form.
4. With the mixer running, start adding the sugar, 125 ml at a time.
5. Continue to mix for 7–10 minutes. The mixture should become white, thick and glossy.
6. When the mixture is very thick and stiff, reduce the speed to low and add the vinegar and sifted cocoa. Mix well and stir in chocolate chips (if using).
7. Spoon the mixture into a piping bag fitted with a large star nozzle (use a no. 885 if adding chocolate chips, otherwise use a no. 856) and pipe meringues onto the greased baking tray, leaving at least 3 cm between them.
8. Bake for 1 hour, then turn off the heat and leave the meringues in the oven for a few hours to cool completely.
9. Store in an airtight container and enjoy on their own, drizzled with chocolate sauce, or with ice cream and berries.

CRUNCHIES

MAKES ABOUT 1.2 KG (35–40)

250 g margarine

30 ml syrup

10 ml bicarbonate of soda

500 ml cake flour

500 ml brown sugar

2.5 ml ground ginger

2.5 ml ground cinnamon

2.5 ml salt

250 ml desiccated coconut

750 ml oats

2 extra-large eggs

1. Preheat the oven to 180 ˚C and spray a 28 x 40 cm baking tray with non-stick cooking spray.
2. Melt the margarine and syrup in a small saucepan. Remove from the heat and add the bicarbonate of soda.
3. Combine all the dry ingredients in a large mixing bowl, add the margarine mixture and eggs and mix well.
4. Spread the mixture onto the greased baking tray and even it out by gently pressing down with the back of a spoon.
5. Bake for 25 minutes, then remove from the oven and leave to cool slightly.
6. Cut into squares while still warm and leave to cool completely in the tray.
7. Store in airtight containers.

Crunchies make an excellent mid-morning snack and a healthy lunchbox treat.

Coffee CREAMS

MAKES 60

175 g cold WoodenSpoon
   yellow margarine
215 ml white sugar
100 ml golden syrup
a pinch of salt
2.5 ml vanilla essence
20 ml dark-roast instant coffee
   granules (I prefer Nescafé)
60 ml cold water
7.5 ml bicarbonate of soda
500 g cake flour
white chocolate buttons to
   decorate (optional)

ICING
375 ml icing sugar
45 g WoodenSpoon yellow
   margarine
7.5 ml dark-roast instant
   coffee granules
20–30 ml water

1. Preheat the oven to 180 ˚C on the thermo-fan setting* and spray a baking tray with non-stick cooking spray.
2. In a large bowl and using an electric mixer, cream the margarine and sugar until pale.
3. Mix in the syrup, followed by the salt and vanilla essence.
4. Dissolve the coffee granules in half the cold water and the bicarbonate of soda in the other half. Add these separately to the mixture. Mix lightly – the mixture will curdle but will come together once the flour has been added.
5. With the mixer running on low speed, add the flour in batches. Beat until well combined.
6. Spoon the dough into a cookie press and fill the greased baking tray with biscuits spaced 3 cm apart.
7. Bake for 12–14 minutes until golden brown.
8. Transfer the biscuits onto a wire cooling rack and bake another batch, continuing until you have used up all the dough. Allow the biscuits to cool completely before icing.
9. To make the icing, beat all the ingredients using an electric mixer on low speed. When combined, increase to high speed and beat until light and fluffy. The icing should be just soft enough to pipe. Spoon the icing into a piping bag fitted with a plain round nozzle.
10. Use a piped teaspoonful of icing to sandwich two biscuits together. If you like, you can pipe a pea-sized amount of icing on top to glue on a chocolate button as decoration.
11. Allow the coffee creams to set for at least 1 hour before storing in an airtight container.

* While a thermo-fan oven is preferable, a conventional oven will also work.

This is my take on the old-fashioned coffee biscuit. They have a distinct coffee flavour.

SOETKOEKIES

MAKES ABOUT 2 KG (110–120)

750 ml white sugar

500 g WoodenSpoon yellow
    margarine

3 large eggs

15 ml baking powder

5 ml salt

1.5 litres cake flour

1. In a large bowl and using an electric mixer, cream the sugar and margarine until pale and fluffy.
2. With the mixer running on low speed, add the eggs one at a time, followed by the baking powder and salt.
3. With the mixer still on low speed, add the flour in batches and mix until well combined.
4. Cover the bowl with cling wrap and refrigerate for at least 30 minutes.
5. Preheat the oven to 180 °C on the thermo-fan setting* and spray a baking tray with non-stick cooking spray.
6. Divide the chilled dough into four portions and form into balls.
7. On a well-floured surface and using a rolling pin, roll out one ball of dough to 2–3 mm thick.
8. Press out biscuits using a flower-shaped cookie cutter.
9. Gently remove the excess dough and lift the biscuits with a cake knife onto the greased baking tray, spacing them 3 cm apart.
10. Bake for 12–14 minutes until light golden in colour. While they are baking, roll out the next ball of dough.
11. Transfer the baked biscuits onto a wire cooling rack and put the next batch in the oven.
12. Continue until you have used up all the dough.
13. Leave the soetkoekies to cool completely before storing in an airtight container.

* While a thermo-fan oven is preferable, a conventional oven will also work.

Soetkoekies are as well known in South Africa as koeksisters, and are simple and inexpensive biscuits to enjoy with tea or coffee. Here you'll find the same favourite taste in a new pattern.

Ginger BISCUITS

MAKES ABOUT 2 KG (75–80)

250 g butter at room
temperature

250 ml golden syrup

750 ml brown sugar

1 ml salt

35 ml ground ginger

30 ml bicarbonate of soda

125 ml milk

750 g cake flour

1. Preheat the oven to 180 °C on a thermo-fan setting* and spray a large baking tray with non-stick cooking spray.
2. In a large mixing bowl and using an electric mixer, beat the butter and syrup, then add 500 ml sugar and mix until pale.
3. With the mixer running on low speed, add the salt and ginger.
4. Dissolve the bicarbonate of soda in the milk and add to the mixture.
5. With the mixer still on low speed, add the flour in batches and mix until well combined.
6. Add 250 ml sugar and mix.
7. Pinch off bits of dough and form into balls each weighing 30 g. Place the balls on the greased baking tray and flatten to 1.5 cm thick with the back of a solid spatula. Make sure there is at least 3 cm of space between each. (In the hot summer months it might not be necessary to press them flat, as the dough will be warmer and spread easier.)
8. Bake for 14–15 minutes until golden.
9. Transfer the biscuits onto a wire cooling rack while you bake the remainder.
10. Cool completely before storing in an airtight container.

* While a thermo-fan oven is preferable, a conventional oven will also work.

I have developed this recipe to be both crunchy and chewy. We like our ginger biscuits a little larger than average.

Gerhard's favourite
CHOCOLATE TREATS

MAKES ABOUT 900 G (35–40)

125 g butter

500 ml white sugar

125 ml cocoa powder, sifted

125 ml milk

750 ml oats

250 ml desiccated coconut

5 ml vanilla essence

1. Grease a large baking tray.
2. Place the butter, sugar, cocoa powder and milk in a large saucepan over medium heat.
3. When it starts to bubble, turn down the heat to medium–low and simmer for exactly 5 minutes, stirring every now and then. The mixture should bubble while simmering.
4. Combine the oats and coconut in a bowl.
5. After 5 minutes, remove the pan from the stove and stir in the vanilla essence.
6. Working quickly, stir in the oats and coconut.
7. Using two tablespoons, place mounds of the mixture, spaced 2 cm apart, onto the greased baking tray. It sets rapidly, so work quickly.
8. Let it set and cool completely before storing in an airtight container in the fridge.

This underestimated chocolate delight is like a healthy fudge. It is my husband Gerhard's favourite chocolate treat.

Creamy
HOMEMADE FUDGE

MAKES 25–30

500 ml white sugar
75 ml water
60 g butter
30 ml golden syrup
385 g can condensed milk
5 ml vanilla essence

1. Grease a small, 25 x 20 cm baking tray.
2. Heat the sugar and water in a medium saucepan over medium heat and stir until the sugar has dissolved.
3. Add the butter and syrup and stir until the butter has melted.
4. Stir in the condensed milk.
5. Turn down the heat to low and cook for 5–10 minutes until the fudge reaches the soft ball stage or turns a caramel colour. (Soft ball stage is when you drop a small amount of fudge into ice water and it forms a soft ball.)
6. Remove the pan from the heat, add the vanilla essence and beat with a wooden spoon for 5 minutes.
7. Pour the fudge onto the greased baking tray and leave it to cool slightly.
8. Cut into squares and cool completely before storing in an airtight container.

White chocolate FRUIT SQUARES

MAKES 550 G (25–30)

250 g white chocolate

100 g glacé cherries, chopped

75 g mixed citrus peel, chopped

75 g dried cranberries, chopped

50 g flaked almonds

1. Grease a 20 cm square baking tin.
2. Melt 200 g of the chocolate in a bowl set over a small saucepan of simmering water.
3. Add the fruit and almonds and mix well.
4. Tip into the greased baking tin and leave to set slightly.
5. Cut into squares in the tin and refrigerate until hard.
6. Melt the remaining 50 g chocolate in a bowl set over a small saucepan of simmering water, remove from heat and drizzle over the squares with a teaspoon.
7. Lift the squares out of the tin and store them in an airtight container in the fridge.

Generosity: If we wish to be fulfilled in our lives, we must share generously with others.

PESTOS, SAUCES AND JAMS

Pesto is a sauce originating from Northern Italy and derives its name from the Genoese word pestâ, which means to pound or crush, in reference to the original method of preparation, with a pestle and mortar. It is traditionally used in pasta dishes as a sauce, but has evolved into a wonderful accompaniment to bread and is often served as a light lunch or starter.

Basil
PESTO

MAKES ABOUT 250 ML

100 g pine nuts

100 g fresh basil leaves (about 3 large handfuls)

125 ml finely grated Parmesan cheese

15 ml chopped fresh garlic

1 ml salt

125 ml + 15 ml extra-virgin olive oil

salt and freshly ground black pepper to taste

1. Roast the pine nuts in a dry frying pan over medium heat and allow to cool.
2. Place the nuts in the food processor and pulse until chopped.
3. Add basil, cheese, garlic and salt and pulse until blended.*
4. With the processor running slowly, add the 125 ml olive oil in a thin stream.
5. Season the pesto with salt and pepper and spoon into a sterilised glass jar with a tight-fitting lid.
6. Cover the pesto with the 15 ml olive oil to prevent it from oxidising and changing colour. Store in the fridge and use within 30 days.

* If you don't have a food processor and are using a blender, first chop the pine nuts alone, and then add the rest of the ingredients and pulse until blended. Slowly add the olive oil in a thin stream while the blender is running. This will take much longer than a food processor.

Basil is such a generous herb. When you plant it, it always delivers a harvest of beautiful leaves and can be preserved by drying or making pesto. Serve on bruschetta with extra grated Parmesan cheese or as a sauce for any pasta.

Sundried tomato
PESTO

MAKES ABOUT 250 ML

125 ml pine nuts

240 g sundried tomatoes in vinaigrette, drained

150 ml finely grated Parmesan cheese

15 ml fresh origanum

15 ml brown sugar

1 ml salt

125 ml + 15 ml extra-virgin olive oil

salt and freshly ground black pepper to taste

1. Roast the pine nuts in a dry frying pan over medium heat and allow to cool.
2. Place the nuts in the food processor and pulse until chopped.
3. Add sundried tomatoes, cheese, origanum, sugar and salt and pulse until blended.*
4. With the processor running slowly, add the 125 ml olive oil in a thin stream.
5. Season the pesto with salt and pepper and spoon into a sterilised glass jar with a tight-fitting lid.
6. Cover the pesto with the 15 ml olive oil to prevent it from oxidising and changing colour. Store in the fridge and use within 30 days.

* If you don't have a food processor and are using a blender, first chop the pine nuts alone, and then add the rest of the ingredients and pulse until blended. Slowly add the olive oil in a thin stream while the blender is running. This will take much longer than a food processor.

This pesto is a sure winner with fresh bread as a starter at any braai or party. Pine nuts are very expensive and can be substituted with blanched almonds.

Sweet MUSTARD

MAKES ABOUT 250 ML

2.5–5 ml hot English mustard powder
50 ml white vinegar
385 g can condensed milk
60 ml Dijon mustard

1. In a small bowl, mix the mustard powder and vinegar.
2. In a medium bowl, combine the condensed milk and Dijon mustard.
3. Add the mustard and vinegar mixture to the larger bowl and mix until combined.
4. Spoon into a glass bottle with a tight-fitting lid.
5. Store in the fridge and use within three months.

My late maternal grandmother, Bessie Keulder, used to make this mustard and the recipe was passed on to me. Serve with gammon and cold meats as a condiment and on meaty sandwiches. The amount of mustard powder can be adjusted to taste.

TARTAR SAUCE

125 ml creamy mayonnaise

1.25 ml hot English mustard powder

60 ml finely chopped chives

30 ml finely chopped fresh parsley

5 ml white sugar

salt and freshly ground black pepper to taste

1. Combine all the ingredients in a small bowl and store in the fridge until needed. Use on the day of making.

No store-bought tartar sauce can compare to this homemade recipe. Serve with fresh-baked fish and seafood.

BÉARNAISE SAUCE

1 small onion, halved

75 ml white wine vinegar

1 bay leaf

6 black peppercorns

3 sprigs fresh parsley

2 egg yolks

125 g butter, cubed

5 ml finely chopped fresh
    mixed herbs

salt and freshly ground black
    pepper to taste

1. Place the onion halves in a small saucepan with the vinegar, bay leaf, peppercorns and parsley.
2. Bring to the boil and then turn down the heat to a simmer. Reduce the liquid to 20 ml.
3. Strain through a sieve and return the liquid to the pan on the stove over low heat.
4. Using a whisk, stir in the egg yolks, one at a time, making sure the sauce does not curdle.
5. Stir in a cube of butter at a time until the sauce thickens and becomes an emulsion.
6. Remove from the heat, add the mixed herbs and season with salt and pepper.
7. Serve warm over steak.

Béarnaise sauce is not commonly known in South Africa. It is a rich, butter-based French sauce that goes very well with fillet, rump and rib-eye steak.

CHEESE SAUCE

100 g butter

200 ml cake flour

1 litre full-cream milk

250 ml grated Cheddar cheese

125 ml grated Parmesan cheese

2.5 ml salt

freshly ground black pepper to taste

1. Melt the butter in a saucepan over medium heat.
2. Add the flour and stir with a whisk until smooth to form a roux.
3. Gradually add the milk, 125 ml at a time, stirring constantly to prevent lumps from forming. Cook the roux until thick and smooth after every addition.
4. Continue to simmer and stir over medium heat until the sauce is thick, smooth and creamy. This should take about 5 minutes.
5. Add the grated cheeses, stir until melted and season with the salt and black pepper to taste.

This cheese sauce can be served on vegetables as well as steak or chicken fillets.

TOMATO BASE
for pizza

15 ml olive oil

5 ml chopped fresh garlic

400 g can chopped tomatoes

5 ml dried origanum

2.5 ml salt

5 ml brown sugar

1. Heat the olive oil in a saucepan and sauté the garlic.
2. Add the remaining ingredients and cook over medium heat, reducing until thick.
3. Blend with an electric handheld blender until smooth.
4. Set aside until needed.

Tomato and
ONION SAUCE

15 ml olive oil

1 large onion, diced

4 medium tomatoes, chopped

30 ml cake flour

60 ml chutney

30 ml tomato sauce

30 ml Worcestershire sauce

5 ml brown sugar

2.5 ml salt

freshly ground black pepper to taste

375 ml water

1. Heat the olive oil in a large frying pan and sauté the onion until soft.
2. Add the tomatoes and sauté until cooked.
3. Stir in the flour, and then add the chutney, tomato sauce and Worcestershire sauce.
4. Stir well, and then add the sugar, salt and black pepper to taste.
5. Add the water and bring to the boil.
6. Turn down the heat and simmer until the sauce is reduced and thick.

There are many versions of this relish available, but I prefer this one, as it is slightly thicker and sweeter. Serve with pap or steak.

Slow-baked creamy brown
MUSHROOM SAUCE

SERVES 6–8

600 g whole brown mushrooms

80 g soft butter

60 ml cake flour

2.5 ml hot English mustard powder

5 ml salt

5 ml chopped fresh thyme

10 ml crushed garlic

1 onion, finely chopped

freshly ground black pepper to taste

250 ml cream

1. Preheat the oven to 180 ˚C.
2. Place the brown mushrooms in a 20-cm diameter and 10-cm deep round ovenproof serving dish.
3. Mix the butter, flour, mustard, salt and thyme and dot the mixture over the mushrooms.
4. Sprinkle over the garlic, followed by the onion, and season with black pepper.
5. Pour over the cream.
6. Bake for 1 hour.
7. If the sauce is too thick, stir in a few tablespoons of milk.
8. Serve warm.

This is so much more than a sauce – it is slow-baked mushrooms at their best! Delicious served with steak.

Tomato JAM

MAKES ABOUT 1.6 LITRES

1 kg cherry tomatoes, halved
1 kg white sugar
1 (2 x 4 cm) root dry ginger
1 ml cream of tartar

1. Sterilise 6–8 (200 ml) clean glass bottles with lids by filling them with boiling water 10 minutes before the jam is cooked. Dry with a clean kitchen towel just before filling.
2. Place the tomatoes in an extra-large saucepan, pour over the sugar and stir.
3. Let it stand for about 90 minutes until the sugar has dissolved.
4. Add the ginger and bring to the boil over medium heat.
5. Wet a pastry brush with water and brush all the excess sugar crystals from the sides of the pan.
6. Simmer over low–medium heat for 50–60 minutes, stirring every 5 minutes.
7. If the jam makes excessive froth, scoop this off with a large spoon.
8. Add the cream of tartar and stir well.
9. Remove the ginger root.
10. Pour the hot jam into the sterilised bottles, filling them to 0.5 cm from the top. Hold the bottle in a kitchen towel so you don't burn yourself and screw the lid on immediately, making sure it is very tight.
11. Label each bottle with a sticker with its name and the date and leave to cool.
12. Store in a cool place. Once opened, it will keep for three months in the fridge.

I started planting cherry tomatoes a few years ago and was surprised by the bumper crops they yield. What do you do when you have too many cherry tomatoes? You make jam! Since I started making this jam, I will never buy tomato jam ever again. I always make sure I have made jam before the end of the season. This jam is slightly runny and has a hint of ginger.

Strawberry JAM

MAKES ABOUT 1.2 LITRES

1 kg strawberries, hulled and halved
1 kg white sugar
1 ml cream of tartar

1. Prepare 5–6 (200 ml) clean glass bottles with lids by filling them with boiling water 10 minutes before the jam is cooked. Dry with a clean kitchen towel just before filling.
2. Cut any overly large strawberries into quarters. Place them all in an extra-large saucepan, pour over the sugar and stir.
3. Let it stand for about 90 minutes until the sugar has dissolved, then bring to the boil over medium heat.
4. Wet a pastry brush with water and brush all the excess sugar crystals from the sides of the pan.
5. Simmer over low–medium heat for 25–30 minutes, stirring every 5 minutes. If the jam makes froth, scoop it off with a large spoon.
6. At the end of cooking, add the cream of tartar and stir well.
7. To test the jam, place a saucer in the freezer for 5 minutes. Pour a teaspoonful of hot jam onto the cold saucer and let it stand for 2 minutes. It should be set slightly to the touch but run slowly when the plate is tilted.
8. Pour the hot jam into the sterilised bottles, filling them to 0.5 cm from the top. Hold the bottle in a kitchen towel so you don't burn yourself and screw the lid on immediately, making sure it is very tight.
9. Label each bottle with a sticker with its name and the date and leave to cool. Store in a cool place. Once opened, it will keep for three months in the fridge.

I prefer jam to be slightly runny. Once opened, this jam should be stored in the fridge. When taken out and used immediately, the cold temperature brings it to the perfect consistency.

Mulberry JAM

1 kg mulberries, stalks removed
1 kg white sugar
1 ml cream of tartar
10 ml lemon juice

1. Prepare 4–5 (200 ml) clean glass bottles with lids by filling them with boiling water 10 minutes before the jam is cooked. Dry with a clean kitchen towel just before filling.
2. Place the mulberries in an extra-large saucepan, pour over the sugar and stir. Let it stand for about 90 minutes until the sugar has dissolved, then bring to the boil over medium heat.
3. Wet a pastry brush with water and brush all the excess sugar crystals from the sides of the pan.
4. Simmer over low–medium heat for 25–30 minutes, stirring every 5 minutes. If the jam makes froth, scoop it off with a large spoon.
5. At the end of cooking, add the cream of tartar and lemon juice and stir well.
6. To test the jam, place a saucer in the freezer for 5 minutes. Pour a teaspoon of hot jam onto the cold saucer and let it stand for 2 minutes. It should be set slightly to the touch but run slowly when the plate is tilted.
7. Pour the hot jam into the sterilised bottles, filling them to 0.5 cm from the top. Hold the bottle in a kitchen towel so you don't burn yourself and screw the lid on immediately, making sure it is very tight.
8. Label each bottle with a sticker with its name and the date and leave to cool. Store in a cool place. Once opened, it will keep for three months in the fridge.

If you have a mulberry tree in your garden, do make this jam. It is quick and easy, and makes a beautiful dark red-wine coloured jam.

CONVERSION CHARTS

GENERAL CONVERSIONS: METRIC TO IMPERIAL

TEASPOONS

Metric	Imperial
2 ml	¼ tsp
2.5 ml	½ tsp
5 ml	1 tsp
10 ml	2 tsp
20 ml	4 tsp

TABLESPOONS

Metric	Imperial
15 ml	1 Tbsp
30 ml	2 Tbsp
45 ml	3 Tbsp
60 ml	4 Tbsp

CUPS

Metric	Imperial
60 ml	¼ cup
80 ml	⅓ cup
125 ml	½ cup
160 ml	⅔ cup
200 ml	¾ cup
250 ml	1 cup
375 ml	1½ cups
500 ml	2 cups
750 ml	3 cups
1 litre	4 cups

INGREDIENT-SPECIFIC CONVERSIONS

BASIC INGREDIENTS

Ingredient	¼ cup = 60 ml	⅓ cup = 80 ml	½ cup = 125 ml	¾ cup = 200 ml	1 cup = 250 ml
Butter			115 g		230 g
Coconut, desiccated	20 g	25 g	40 g	65 g	80 g
Flour: cake, self-raising, white or brown bread, wholewheat	35 g	45 g	70 g	110 g	140 g
Raisins, sultanas	40 g	50 g	75 g	120 g	150 g
Sugar: castor	50 g	70 g	105 g	170 g	210 g
Sugar: granulated (white or brown)	50 g	65 g	100 g	160 g	200 g
Sugar: icing	35 g	45 g	65 g	100 g	130 g

OTHER INGREDIENTS

Ingredient	Grams per 1 cup = 250 ml	Ingredient	Grams per 1 cup = 250 ml
Biscuit crumbs	120 g	Nuts, grated	100 g
Chocolate chips	200 g	Nuts, chopped or slivered	150 g
Cornflour	120 g	Nuts, whole	100 g
Dates	150 g	Oats, rolled	80 g

INDEX